Workshop on Cognitive Modeling and Computational Linguistics (CMCL 2020)

Online
19 November 2020

ISBN: 978-1-7138-1991-2

CMCL 2020

The Workshop on Cognitive Modeling and Computational Linguistics

Proceedings of the Workshop

November 19, 2020
Online event

Introduction

Welcome to the Workshop on Cognitive Modeling and Computational Linguistics (CMCL)!

Since the early editions, CMCL has been a reference point for the research at the intersection between Computational Linguistics and Cognitive Science. The edition of this year, because of the COVID-19 pandemic, will not be held in Punta Cana as we originally planned, but it will be the first to be held entirely online. Despite this, we still received 17 regular paper submissions and 10 were accepted for publication (the total acceptance rate is 58%, the same of the 2019 edition), proving that CMCL is followed by a strong and active research community. We also received 2 cross-submissions, and we accepted one for presentation at the workshop.

The program of this year is rich, stimulating and diversified, with topics ranging from language acquisition to models of linguistic alignment and language disorders. We would like to deeply thank all the reviewers of our PC, without whom we would not have been able to select the best papers for our program.

We also thank Prof Suzanne Stevenson and Prof Richard Futrell, for having accepted our invitation to deliver the keynote speeches.

Finally, thanks to our sponsors, we were able to offer registration fee waivers to PhD students and to offset the costs of participation of the invited speakers: we gratefully acknowledge support from the Laboratoire Parole et Langage (LPL), Aix-en-Provence (France) and from the Japan Society for the Promotion of Science.

Organizers:

Emmanuele Chersoni (Hong Kong Polytechnic University)
Cassandra Jacobs (University of Wisconsin)
Yohei Oseki (University of Tokyo)
Laurent Prévot (Aix-Marseille University)
Enrico Santus (Bayer)

Program Committee:

Laura Aina (Pompeu Fabre University of Barcelona)
Raquel Garrido Alhama (Max Planck Institute for Psycholinguistics)
Afra Alishahi (Tilburg University)
Philippe Blache (Aix-Marseille University)
Christos Christodoulopoulos (Amazon)
Aniello De Santo (University of Utah)
Micha Elsner (Ohio State University)
Raquel Fernandez (University of Amsterdam)
Abdellah Fourtassi (Aix-Marseille University)
Thomas Francois (Catholic University of Louvain)
Robert Frank (Yale University)
John Hale (University of Georgia)
Anna Ivanova (MIT)
Yu-Yin Hsu (Hong Kong Polytechnic University)
Tim Hunter (UCLA)
Samar Husain (IIT Delhi)
Shalom Lappin (University of Gothenburg)
Gianluca Lebani (University Ca' Foscari Venezia)
Fred Mailhot (DialPad)
Syrielle Montariol (University of Paris Sud – LIMSI CNRS)
Karl Neergaard (University of Macau)
Stephen Politzer-Ahles (Hong Kong Polytechnic University)
Vito Pirrelli (ILC-CNR Pisa)
Carlos Ramisch (Aix-Marseille University)
Giulia Rambelli (University of Pisa)
Roi Reichart (Technion – Israel Institute of Technology)
Rachel A Ryskin (MIT)
William Schuler (Ohio State University)
Marina Sedinkina (University of Munich)
Olga Seminck (Catholic University of Louvain)
Marco Silvio Giuseppe Senaldi (McGill University)
Cory Shain (Ohio State University)
Aaron Steven White (University of Rochester)
Victoria Yaneva (University of Wolverhampton)
Yao Yao (Hong Kong Polytechnic University)
Frances Yung (Saarland University)

Invited Speakers:

Richard Futrell (University of California Irvine)
Suzanne Stevenson (University of Toronto)

Table of Contents

Conference Program

November 19, 2020

9:30–9:45   **Introduction**

9:45–10:45   **Keynote Talk**

How Languages Carve Up the World: Cognitive Explanation through Computational Modeling
Suzanne Stevenson

10:45–11:15   **Break**

11:15–12:15   **Session 1: Oral Presentations**

What Determines the Order of Verbal Dependents in Hindi? Effects of Efficiency in Comprehension and Production
Kartik Sharma, Richard Futrell and Samar Husain

Images and Imagination: Automated Analysis of Priming Effects Related to Autism Spectrum Disorder and Developmental Language Disorder
Michaela Regneri, Diane King, Fahreen Walji and Olympia Palikara

12:15–13:30   **Lunch Break**

13:30–13:45   **Poster Booster**

13:45–14:45   **Poster Session**

Production-based Cognitive Models as a Test Suite for Reinforcement Learning Algorithms
Adrian Brasoveanu and Jakub Dotlacil

Evaluating Word Embeddings for Language Acquisition
Raquel G. Alhama, Caroline Rowland and Evan Kidd

Guessing the Age of Acquisition of Italian Lemmas through Linear Regression
Irene Russo

Word Co-occurrence in Child-directed Speech Predicts Children's Free Word Associations
Abdellah Fourtassi

Development of Multi-level Linguistic Alignment in Child-adult Conversations
Thomas Misiek, Benoit Favre and Abdellah Fourtassi

Conditioning, but on Which Distribution? Grammatical Gender in German Plural Inflection
Kate McCurdy, Adam Lopez and Sharon Goldwater

Probabilistic Weighting of Perspectives in Dyadic Communication (cross-submission)
Rachel A Ryskin, Suzanne Stevenson, Daphna Heller

Pressures on Language Emergence: Least Effort, Object Constancy and Frequency (Findings of EMNLP)
Diana Rodriguez Luna, Edoardo Maria Ponti, Dieuwke Hupkes, Elia Bruni

Inferring Symmetry in Natural Language (Findings of EMNLP)
Chelsea Tanchip, Lei Yu, Aotao Xu, Yang Xu

14:45–15:45   Session 2: Oral Presentations

15:45–16:45   Keynote Talk

16:45–17:00   Closing Remarks

What determines the order of verbal dependents in Hindi? Effects of efficiency in comprehension and production

Kartik Sharma[†], Richard Futrell[‡*] and Samar Husain[†*]
[†]Indian Institute of Technology Delhi, [‡]University of California Irvine
kartik.sharma.cs117@cse.iitd.ac.in, rfutrell@uci.edu,
samar@iitd.ac.in

Abstract

Word order flexibility is one of the distinctive features of SOV languages. In this work we investigate whether the order and relative distance of preverbal dependents in Hindi, an SOV language, is affected by factors motivated by efficiency considerations during language comprehension and production. We investigate the influence of Head–Dependent Mutual Information (HDMI), similarity-based interference, accessibility and case-marking. Results show that preverbal dependents remain close to the verbal head when the HDMI between the verb and its dependent is high. This demonstrates the influence of locality constraints on dependency distance and word order in an SOV language. Additionally, dependency distance were found to be longer when the dependent was animate, when it was case-marked and when it was semantically similar to other preverbal dependents. Together the results highlight the cross-linguistic generalizability of these factors and provide evidence for a functionally motivated account of word order in SOV languages such as Hindi.

1 Introduction

Natural languages are known to be influenced by a pressure for efficiency, that is, languages should enable speakers to communicate as well as possible, subject to constraints on the complexity of production and comprehension (Zipf, 1949; Jaeger and Tily, 2011; Gibson et al., 2019; Hawkins, 2014). One area where efficiency pressures appear to have a large effect is in word order: for example, across languages, the distribution of word orders can be well predicted using the principle of dependency length minimization, the idea that words in syntactic dependencies are under a pressure to be close to each other (Liu et al., 2017; Temperley and Gildea,

2018). Dependency length minimization is motivated by efficiency because it results in lower working memory requirements for language production and comprehension.

Here, we take up the question of whether word orders can be predicted using efficiency in an area that goes beyond dependency length minimization. In particular, we examine how efficiency pressures may influence the order of pre-verbal dependencies in a verb-final language, Hindi. We formalize a number of measures of the complexity of comprehension and production, drawing from the psycholinguistic literature, and we test what effect these measures have on word order as observed in a large dependency treebank.

The paper is arranged as follows: in Section 2, we describe the various psycholinguistic factors used to investigate preverbal ordering and review related work. Section 3 describes the data and methods used to undertake the various analyses. In Section 4 we present the results. Section 5 discusses the implications of our results and concludes.

2 Psycholinguistic Factors influencing Word Order

We consider four psycholinguistically-motivated factors as predictors of the order of verbal dependents in Hindi.

Head–dependent mutual information (HDMI)
While the theory of dependency length minimization holds that all words in dependencies should be close to each other, there is no theoretical consensus on *which* words in dependencies should be especially close to each other. In contrast, the more general theory of **information locality** holds that any two words w_1 and w_2 should be close to each other in proportion to their **pointwise mutual in-**

---

*Equal contribution by RF and SH.

Proceedings of the Workshop on Cognitive Modeling and Computational Linguistics, pages 1–10
Online Event, November 19, 2020. ©2020 Association for Computational Linguistics
https://doi.org/10.18653/v1/P17

formation (pmi):

$$\text{pmi}(w_1; w_2) \equiv \log \frac{p(w_1, w_2)}{p(w_1)p(w_2)}. \quad (1)$$

In support of this idea, in previous work, Futrell (2019) found that dependencies in which the head and dependent have high pmi are under a stronger pressure to be close than dependencies with less head–dependent mutual information.

The idea of information locality is motivated by efficiency in language comprehension, based on information-theoretic models of incremental sentence processing. For example, the model of Futrell et al. (2020b) holds that the difficulty of processing a word in context is given by the surprisal (negative log probability) of the word given a lossy memory representation of the context. Information locality can be derived as a consequence of this model.

Following previous work, we operationalize the head–dependent mutual information as the pointwise mutual information between part-of-speech tags. Our main reason for using the pmi between part-of-speech tags, rather than the pmi between wordforms, is in order to avoid data sparsity issues in the estimation of mutual information (Paninski, 2003; Futrell et al., 2019). However, this choice also changes the interpretation of the HDMI measure. Instead of reflecting the full predictive information contained in one word about another word, the measure now only reflects something like the *syntactic* predictive information contained in one word about another.

For representing words for this measure, we use an augmented part-of-speech tagset described in Section 3.2.1. This tagset captures not only part-of-speech information, but also verb argument structure and nominal case marking.

Accessibility A persistent generalization in the typological literature is that there is a bias for words which are more **accessible** to go earlier in a sentence. Words are more accessible when they are animate, definite, imageability, and/or salient in discourse (Ariel, 1990; Jaeger and Tily, 2011). The preference for more accessible words to go earlier in sentences appears to be motivated by ease of language production (Ferreira and Dell, 2000; Kurumada and Jaeger, 2015), under the theory that language producers will tend to produce the words which are most accessible as quickly as possible. Evidence for production ease comes from, amongst others, the observation that lemma selection during grammatical encoding is influenced by accessibility of the lemma (e.g., Bock and Warren, 1985; Bock et al., 1992; Prat-Sala and Branigan, 2000; Branigan et al., 2008).

Here we operationalize accessibility as the animacy of a referent. We leave investigations of other factors affecting accessibility (definiteness, imageability, etc.) to future work.

Semantic similarity A great deal of work in psycholinguistics has focused on the effect of **similarity-based interference** on processing: the idea that difficulty results when a comprehender must retrieve a target item from working memory, but there is another distractor item in working memory which interferes with the retrieval of the target item (Jäger et al., 2017). From a production perspective, presence of similar phrases in an utterance can lead to competition between the phrases and thereby difficulty in planning. Successful articulation of a phrase therefore requires inhibition of one of the phrases, thereby resulting in a delayed articulation of the inhibited phrase. The magnitude of this interference increases as the target and the distractor become more similar (Gordon et al., 2006; Gennari et al., 2012). For comprehension, this effect has been modeled within frameworks based on cue-based retrieval such as ACT-R (Lewis and Vasishth, 2005).

In terms of word order, it has been shown that when syntactically/semantically similar nominals appear adjacent (or close) to each other, processing suffers (e.g., Lewis and Nakayama, 2002; Vasishth, 2003; Gordon et al., 2006; Apurva and Husain, 2020). Relatedly, there has been some work on the influence of semantic interference during production (e.g., Ferreira and Firato, 2002; Humphreys et al., 2016; Gennari et al., 2012; MacDonald, 2013). For example, Gennari et al. (2012) found that an animate head noun leads to a higher chance for producing passive relative clause construction in English, compared to an active relative clause, thus keeping the animate head noun distant from the animate passive subject. On this account, a pre-verbal dependent that is similar to other phrases should appear earlier in the sentence because increased dependency distance between similar nouns should lead to production ease.

Therefore, the prediction based on psycholinguistics is that a word should be pushed out towards the beginning of the sentence when it is semantically similar with other words. This creates distance between the two similar words and facilitates language production and comprehension.

Morphological marking A feature of a majority of head-final languages is the presence of case marking on nouns that signifies the syntactic relation between a nouns and its verbal head.[2] Cross-linguistically, the presence of case-markers has been shown to increase the dependency distance between a nominal and its verbal head (e.g., Yadav et al., 2020), perhaps because nominal case-markers help in making robust predictions about upcoming verbs, as shown by Husain et al. (2014). Therefore, we predict that nominals with case marking should be farther out from the verb than those without.

2.1 Related Work

There have been some previous corpus-based investigations on word order variation in Hindi (e.g., Husain et al., 2013; Ranjan et al., 2019); (also see, Vasishth, 2004). For example, Ranjan et al. (2019) investigated the role of case-marking on word order choices in Hindi and found evidence for the Easy-First and Reduce Inference principles of the Production Distribution and Comprehension (PDC) hypothesis (MacDonald, 2013). Production ease was operationalized in Ranjan et al. (2019) as low n-gram/dependency surprisal value (Hale, 2001) and interference was operationalized as case-marker similarity between preverbal nominals. Jain et al. (2018) investigated the Uniform Information Density hypothesis (Jaeger, 2010) with regard to predicting Hindi word order in corpus sentences vs random sentences and found no support for UID in capturing such a distinction. They also did not find UID to predict non-canonical word order in Hindi.

With regard to ordering of co-siblings in dependency trees, Dyer (2018) has argued that the relative predictability of the head at the dependent (which can be operationalized as the entropy of heads given dependents) determines which sibling is closer to the head. In particular, he shows that co-siblings that induce lower entropy tend to be closer to the head compared to co-siblings that induce higher entropy. The current work will complement the above investigations by exploring the role of some novel factors such as HDMI, semantic interference, and animacy. The effect of these factors on preverbal ordering and dependency distance in SOV languages is largely unknown.

3 Methodology

3.1 Data and Tools

We use the monolingual Hindi corpus developed by Kunchukuttan et al. (2017). This corpus includes raw sentences of Hindi, collected from various sources (HindMonoCorp (Bojar et al., 2014), BBC, Wikipedia etc.). We restricted our analysis[3] to only the first 5 million sentences of this data, resulting in a dataset of 14 million verbal dependencies. Since we needed to extract noun–verb dependency relations, we parsed this data using the ISC dependency parser for Hindi.[4] The parser is trained on the Hyderabad Dependency Treebank (Bhatt et al., 2009) that is based on the Computational Paninian Grammar (CPG, henceforth) (Bharati et al., 1995).

3.2 Model

In this section, we provide details regarding the computation of the factors discussed in Section 2.

3.2.1 HDMI

As mentioned in Section 2, we calculate the point-wise mutual information between words using augmented part-of-speech tags. Here, we describe the augmentation in detail. A verb is identified with its verb class. Verbal classes are defined based on the different argument structures that a verb can have. A class of a verb is characterized by the set of core argument relations (Subject, Noun complement for Copula, Direct Object, Indirect Object). For example, two verbs will belong to the same class if the set of the core argument relations they have is identical. Thus, we classify a verb into one of the 16 classes according to this scheme. A 16 way classification is based on Sharma et al. (2019). This constitutes an exhaustive set of possible argument structures a verb can have, considering only the core-arguments.

A verb POS tag (*VM*) is augmented with the verb class that it belongs to. Nominal POS tags (*NN*—Common noun, *NNP*—Proper noun) are augmented by case-marker information (if any).

---

[2]Lexically, these case-markers can either appear as a suffix or as an independent token.

[3]All the code has been made available: `https://github.com/Ksartik/Dep_Order_Hindi`

[4]The parser is an implementation of the incremental transition-based arc-eager parsing algorithm (Nivre, 2008). The parser is reported to have a UAS of 93.52% and a LAS of 87.77% (Bhat, 2017). `https://bitbucket.org/account/user/iscnlp/projects/ISCNLP`.

3.2.2 Semantic Similarity

Semantic similarity of a noun in its context is modeled as the maximum cosine similarity (Salton, 1972) of the noun with other pre-verbal dependents of the corresponding verb. The cosine similarity is calculated from the word vectors taken from a pre-trained model for Hindi (Grave et al., 2018). Semantic similarity is

$$\text{sim}(d) = \max_{\substack{d':(h,d')\in\text{Dep} \\ id(d')<id(h)}} \frac{wv(d) \cdot wv(d')}{\|wv(d)\| \, \|wv(d')\|}, \quad (2)$$

where $wv(x)$ denotes the word vector of a word X, $id(x)$ denotes the index of X in the sentence, and $(h, d) \in$ Dep. Note that Dep is the set of all dependencies in the sentence.

We choose to use word vectors to generate similarity scores because collecting human judgments for all words in our large dataset is impractical. There is mixed evidence about whether semantic similarity as defined using word vectors truly captures psycholinguistically relevant aspects of similarity. Despite arguments that word vectors do not capture certain properties of human similarity judgments (Griffiths et al., 2007; De Deyne et al., 2016) and certain semantic interference effects (Merlo and Ackermann, 2018), they have been used successfully in psycholinguistic models of interference (Smith and Vasishth, 2020).

3.2.3 Accessibility

In the current study, the accessibility of a noun is determined based on the notion of humanness. Nouns that are +Human as assumed to have conceptual prominence while nouns with a -Human feature are assumed to have low conceptual prominence. Thus, this is a categorical variable in our study. Animacy information was obtained from hand annotations in a version of the Hyderabad Dependency Treebank augmented with nominal semantic features (Jena et al., 2013). In this text, animate will be used interchangeably for +Human, unless otherwise specified.

3.2.4 Case Marking

The information regarding nominal case-marking is extracted from the parsed data using the DEPREL tag. A noun is case-marked if it has a dependent with DEPREL equal to *lwg__psp* in CPG. Thus, we mark a noun-verbal dependency as case-marked if the corresponding noun is case-marked, otherwise it is deemed unmarked.

3.3 Granularity of Analysis

In order to get a fine-grained view of the data, we will separately analyze the four different relation types: subjects, direct objects, indirect objects, and adjuncts. We label a relation as a subject if its DEPREL tag is either *k1* or *k1s*, as a direct object if it is *k2*, as an indirect object if it is *k4*, and as a verbal adjunct otherwise.

For all analyses, we consider only dependencies with length greater than 1. This is necessary because in Hindi there cannot be any noun-verb dependency at distance 1 when the noun is case-marked—a case-marker appears post-nominally and is adjacent to the noun. Since case-marker is a factor in our analysis, any real effect may be confounded by this constraint of the grammar.

4 Results

In this section we discuss the length and ordering of preverbal nominal dependencies. We first discuss how the length is affected by the factors discussed above. We then discuss how they affect the word-order.

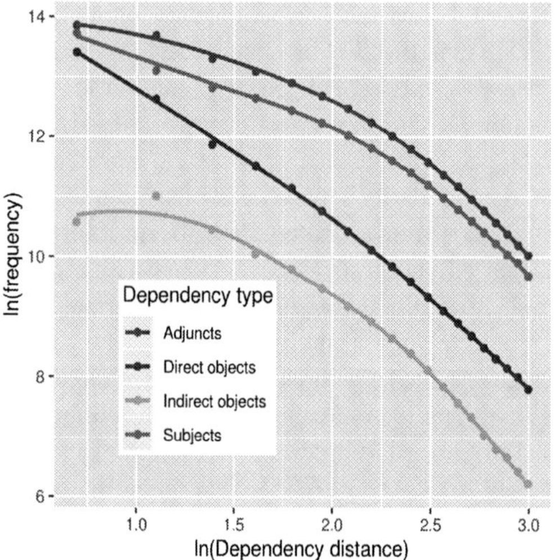

Figure 1: Frequency of various arguments at different dependency distance in logarithmic scale

4.1 Length of Preverbal Dependencies

Figure 1 shows the distribution of dependency distance (the number of words from the head to the dependent) for various arguments in a log–log plot. We find that verbal adjuncts are more frequent than all the arguments at all distances. Among the arguments, subjects are the most frequent at almost all distances followed by direct objects and then indirect objects. With increasing distances, the frequencies of all dependencies decrease but the decay is strikingly slower in subjects and adjuncts compared to the objects. Direct objects decrease steadily following a power law while the others show a nonlinear trend until large distances (> 12).

We now investigate the effect of our psycholinguistically-motivated factors on dependency distance. Figure 2a shows a plot for HDMI at various dependency distances. The trend for preverbal subjects is quite clear: as dependency distance increases, HDMI decreases.

The figure unexpectedly shows that the HDMI for adjuncts and indirect object tends to increase starting around dependency distance 7. One possible reason for this increase is estimation error in the pmi values: given small amounts of data from a relatively large number of classes, pmi is likely to be overestimated (Futrell et al., 2019), and the frequency of these dependents is less at higher dependency distance. Therefore, the HDMI – dependency distance relation for these dependents seems to be more stable at shorter dependency distance. Another explanation for the apparent HDMI increase at large dependency distances could have to do with certain discourse-related dependencies between verbs and adjuncts, where the adjunct appears preferentially at the beginning of a clause or sentence (Butt and King, 1996). Such discourse dependencies might have high HDMI while also having large dependency distance due do the constraint of appearing early.

Figure 2b shows a plot for mean semantic similarity at various dependency distance. We find that for all the arguments, an increase in semantic similarity leads to increase in dependency distance. Figure 2c shows a plot for proportion of animate arguments at various dependency distance. The most clear trend is for the subjects – the proportion of +Human subjects tend to increase with increase in dependency distance. This positive trend is also seen for the other dependents, but for short distances.

Finally, Figure 2d shows a plot for proportion of case-marked arguments at various dependency distance. Here again, the expected positive trend, i.e., an increase in case-marked arguments with increasing length, is seen only for subjects. For direct objects and adjuncts, this trend is reversed. In fact, the negative trend of fewer case-marked

nominals at longer dependency distance is quite strong for direct objects. Note that indirect objects are always case-marked.

In order to quantify the effects of our predictors, we fit a linear regression predicting dependency distance as a function of our predictors:

$$\text{distance} \approx \beta_0 + \beta_1 \times \text{HDMI} + \beta_2 \times \text{Similarity} + \beta_3 \times \text{Animacy} + \beta_4 \times \text{Case} \quad (3)$$

The above model was fit separately for all 4 relations (subject, direct object, indirect object, and adjunct). The variables HDMI and similarity are continuous. On the other hand, the variables animacy and case are categorical in nature. Based on the discussion in Section 2, we expect β_1 to be negative, i.e., dependency distance is expected to decrease with increase in HDMI. The coefficients β_2, β_3 and β_4 are expected to have positive values. In other words, dependency distance is expected to increase when there is increased semantic similarity between nouns, when the argument is +Human and when it is case-marked.

Coefficient	S	DO	IO	Adjuncts
Intercept	-0.19	1.18	0.13	-0.60
HDMI	-0.43	3.50	-0.88	-1.69
Similarity	0.01	0.06	0.02	0.07
Animacy	0.07	0.003	0.03	0.03
Case	1.50	-0.35	—	0.66

Table 1: Linear regression coefficients predicting distance for different dependency types; see Eq. 3. S = Subject; DO = Direct Object; IO = Indirect Object. Variables are centered. Note that case is excluded as a factor for indirect objects.

The values of the fitted coefficients β are shown in Table 1. All coefficients are significant at $p < .05$. For the subjects, adjuncts and indirect objects, we find that all the coefficients are in the expected direction. On the other hand, mirroring the unexpected effects visible in Figure 2, the coefficients of HDMI and case-marker for direct objects[5] are not in the expected direction.

---

[5] At first glance this might seem inconsistent with the distribution of Object and case-marker in Husain et al. (2013) who report that objects closer to the verb are more likely to be bare compared to when they are further away. However, note that Husain et al. (2013) report the overall count, while here we show the proportion at each dependency distance. The trend reported in Husain et al. (2013) can be driven by short dependencies (which form the bulk of all instances); the pattern can, in fact, be seen in Figure 2d for dependency lengths 2-5.

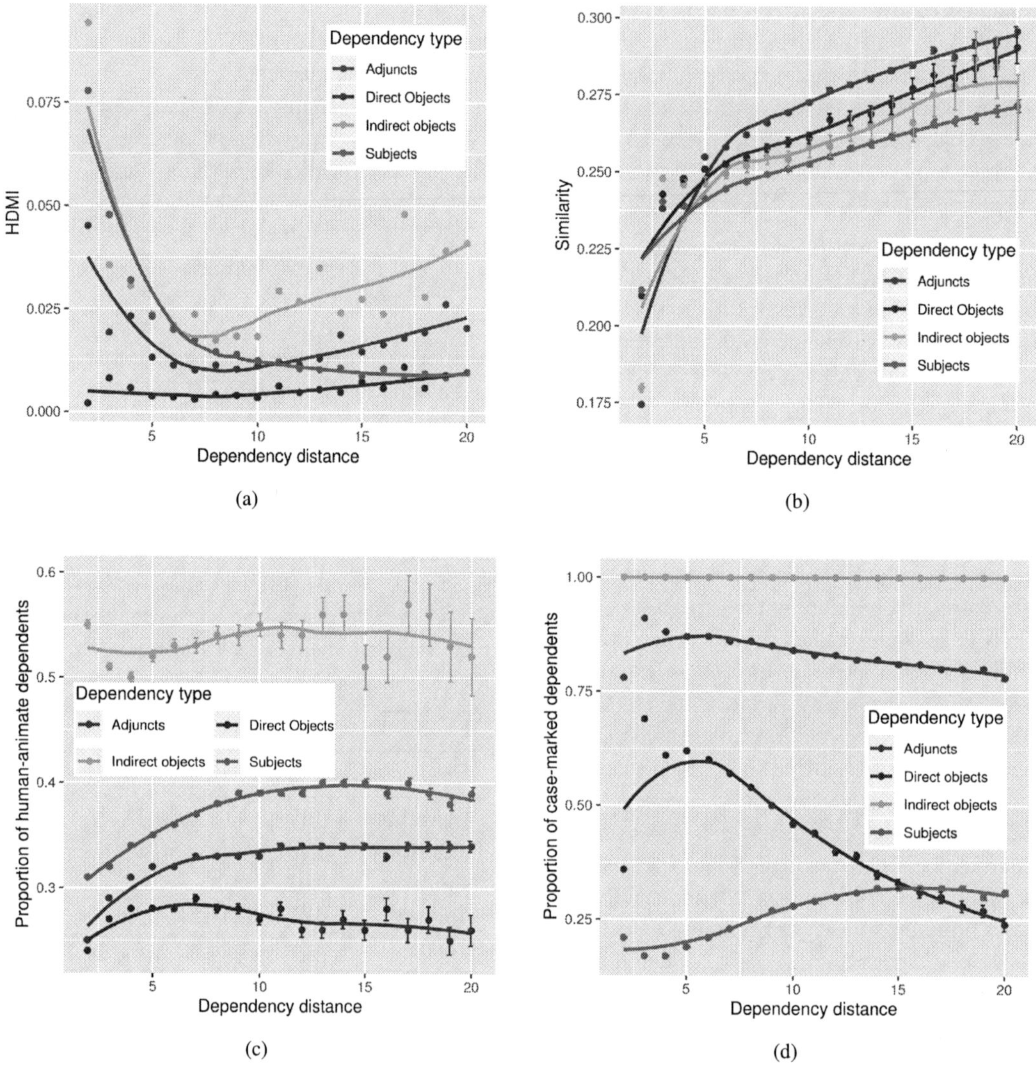

Figure 2: Distribution of factors (mean and 95% CI) at different distances greater than 1.

4.2 Order of Preverbal Dependencies

We now consider how different dependencies of a verb are ordered relative to each other. We consider order between 3 pairs of constituents: (i) arguments and adjuncts, (ii) subjects and objects, and (iii) direct objects and indirect objects. Note that objects constitute both direct objects and indirect objects, and arguments constitute both subjects and objects.

All nominal dependencies attached to a common verb were collected and grouped into the above-mentioned pairs according to their dependency relations. Then, the order between the constituents is calculated by considering the sign of the difference between their dependency distances. Henceforth, we denote an order between constituents X and Y

as X–Y if X precedes Y and Y–X otherwise.

We fit a logistic regression predicting the order of two dependents given the *difference* in the values of the factors for the two dependents (as in Morgan and Levy, 2016; Futrell et al., 2020a). The factors are same as used in the previous section. In particular, we find coefficients β to fit

$$\log \frac{P(X\text{–}Y \text{ order})}{P(Y\text{–}X \text{ order})} \approx \beta_0 + \beta_1 \times \Delta\text{HDMI}$$
$$+ \beta_2 \times \Delta\text{Similarity} + \beta_3 \times \Delta\text{Animacy}$$
$$+ \beta_4 \times \Delta\text{Case}, \qquad (4)$$

where ΔHDMI indicates the HDMI of X minus the HDMI of Y, etc. This model is evaluated separately for argument (X) and adjunct (Y), subject

6

(X) and object (Y), and direct object (X) and indirect object (Y), along with random intercepts by sentence.

Based on the discussion in Section 2, we expect β_1 to be negative, since a higher value of HDMI of X than Y should imply that X is closer to the verb than Y, i.e. the order should be $Y - X$. The similarity coefficient β_2 is expected to be positive based on the effect of interference on distance seen in Section 4.1, and β_3 and β_4 are also expected to have positive values. In other words, a dependent is expected to be farther away from the verb than another dependent when it is more +Human (and case-marked) than the other dependent.

The values of the fitted regression coefficients β are shown in Table 2. Significance is according to the criterion $p < .05$. All effects except ΔSimilarity are in the theoretically expected directions. Figure 3 shows the effect of each factor on the word-order. One can verify the trends with the sign of the coefficients in the regression.

Coefficient	Arg–Adj	S–O	DO–IO
Intercept	0.03	2.32	-1.96
Δ HDMI	-0.99	-1.26	-1.95
Δ Similarity	-0.11	-0.09	0.01[a]
Δ Animacy	0.21	0.16	0.11
Δ Case	1.25	1.50	0.57

[a]Not significant

Table 2: Logistic regression coefficients predicting $X-Y$ vs. $Y-X$ order based on the difference in predictor values for X and Y (see Eq. 4). S = Subject; O = Object, DO = Direct Object; IO = Indirect Object.

5   Discussion

The results show that comprehension/production efficiency based factors affect dependency distance and ordering of preverbal dependents in Hindi.

Previous work investigating dependency distance has demonstrated that SOV languages allow for longer dependency distance between the verb and its prior dependents (Futrell et al., 2020c; Yadav et al., 2020; Konieczny, 2000). The current work makes an important contribution by highlighting that compared to preverbal adjuncts, the core arguments (subject, indirect object and direct object) tend to be closer to the verb in an SOV language like Hindi. Additionally, when the HDMI between the preverbal dependent and the verb is high, they tend to be close to each other. The HDMI difference between a pair of dependencies also correctly predicts their order. This provides compelling evidence that, all else being equal, the preverbal dependents in an SOV language such as Hindi are under information-theoretic locality constraints. Indeed, recent behavioral studies (e.g., Apurva and Husain, 2020) suggest that clause final verb prediction in Hindi suffers with increased distance between prior arguments and the upcoming verb.

The current findings also highlight certain conditions under which locality constraints can be overridden, leading to increased distance between preverbal arguments and the verb. These factors relate to well established processing constraints such as animacy-driven accessibility and similarity-based interference. Language-specific characteristics also influence syntactic configurations. In the current study, the presence of nominal case-markers tends to increase the dependency distance between the verb and its prior dependents. This could highlight the predictive strength of case-markers vis-à-vis a verb type (Husain et al., 2014; Vasishth and Husain, 2014). Under such a setting, the locality constraint can be violated, leading to longer dependency distance.

The results also raise some inconsistencies. One such inconsistency was that the dependency distance prediction for factors such as HDMI and case-marking in the case of direct object is not borne out. It is possible that compared to other arguments, the relationship between a direct object and verb is distinct (Momma and Ferreira, 2019). If this is true, then we should be able to replicate the DO pattern found in the current study for other SOV languages. The other inconsistency in the result was that the prediction for word order with respect to similarity-based interference turned out to be incorrect in the order-based analyses.

The current work does not probe the effect of discourse/information structure on word order. Butt and King (1996) have proposed a discourse-centric mapping of word position vis-à-vis the verb and discourse function – Topic maps to the sentence initial position, Focus maps to the immediate preverbal position, Background Information maps to the postverbal position and Completive Information maps to the non-immediate preverbal position. Such information structure roles can be difficult to ascertain automatically, but future work can attempt to investigate the role of these factors in the

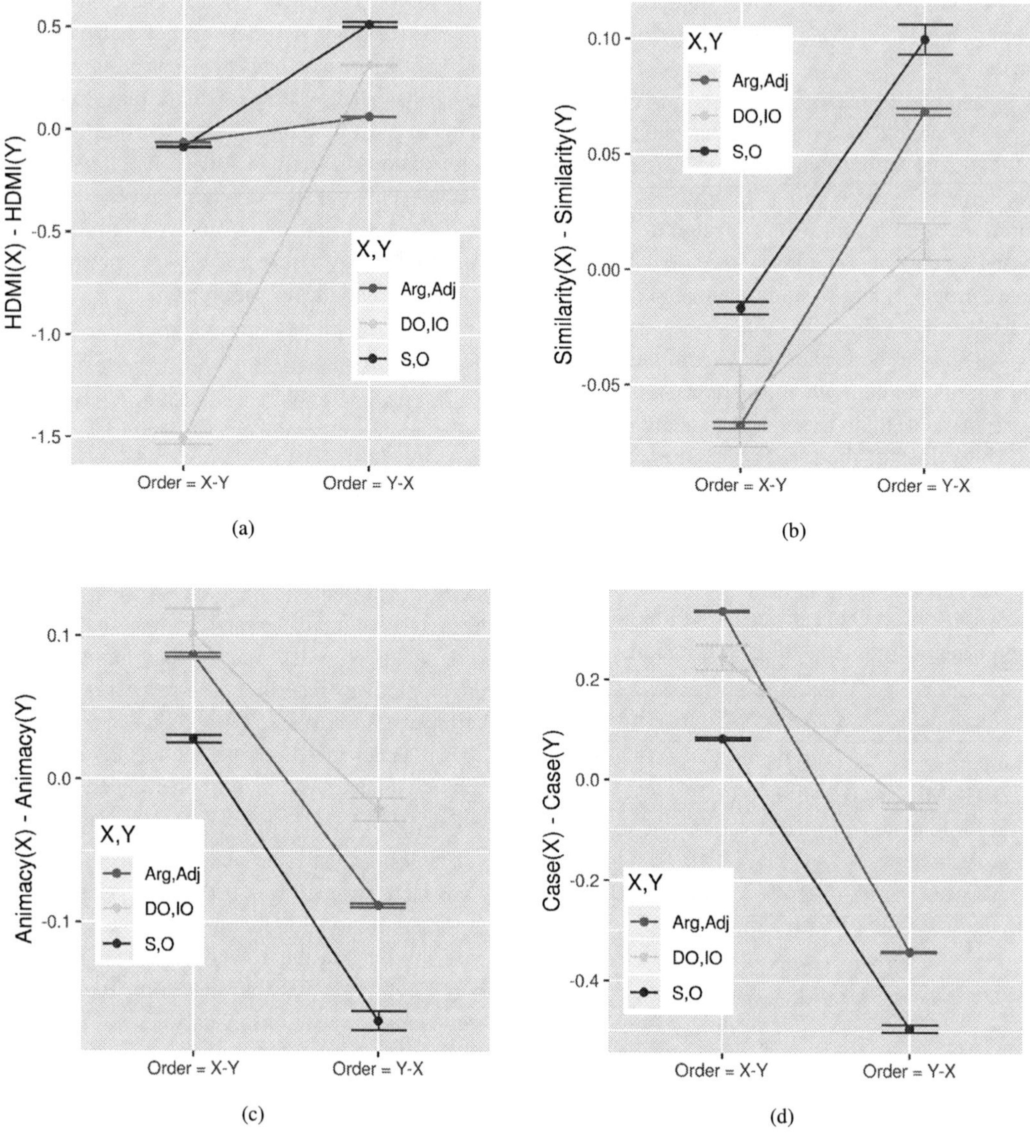

Figure 3: Effect of factors (mean and 95% CI) on the order between constituents X and Y. Arg=Argument; Adj=Adjunct; S=Subject; O=Object, DO=Direct Object; IO=Indirect Object.

context of the current work.

6 Conclusion

Our work provides evidence in support of the information locality hypothesis which states that head-dependent are under pressure to be close to each other when they are strongly associated with each other. It also supports other efficiency-driven factors such as similarity-based interference, accessibility, and the presence of case-markers, which act as countervailing forces to keep the distance between the dependent and its verbal head long.

Together these factors influence the dependency distance and word order patterns in an SOV language like Hindi.

Acknowledgments

We thank the three reviewers for helpful comments.

References

Apurva and Samar Husain. 2020. Parsing errors in hindi: Investigating limits to verbal prediction in an sov language. *In submission.*

Mira Ariel. 1990. *Accessing noun-phrase antecedents.* Routledge.

A. Bharati, V. Chaitanya, and R. Sangal. 1995. *Natural Language Processing: A Paninian Perspective*. Prentice-Hall of India, New Delhi.

Riyaz Bhat. 2017. *Exploiting Linguistic Knowledge to Address Representation and Sparsity Issues in Dependency Parsing of Indian Languages*. Ph.D. thesis, IIIT Hyderabad India.

Rajesh Bhatt, Bhuvana Narasimhan, Martha Palmer, Owen Rambow, Dipti Misra Sharma, and Fei Xia. 2009. A multi-representational and multi-layered treebank for Hindi/Urdu. In *Proceedings of the Third Linguistic Annotation Workshop*.

J. Kathryn Bock, Helga Loebell, and Randal Morey. 1992. From conceptual roles to structural relations: Bridging the syntactic cleft. *Psychological Review*, 99:150 – 171.

J. Kathryn Bock and R. K. Warren. 1985. Conceptual accessibility and syntactic structure in sentence formulation. *Cognition*, 21:47–67.

Ondřej Bojar, Vojtěch Diatka, Pavel Rychlý, Pavel Straňák, Vít Suchomel, Aleš Tamchyna, and Daniel Zeman. 2014. HindEnCorp - Hindi-English and Hindi-only Corpus for Machine Translation. In *Proceedings of LREC'14*.

Holly P. Branigan, Martin J. Pickering, and Mikihiro Tanaka. 2008. Contributions of animacy to grammatical function assignment and word order during production. *Lingua*, 118(2):172 – 189.

M. Butt and T. C. King. 1996. Structural topic and focus without movement. In *M. Butt and T. H. King, eds., The First LFG Conference. CSLI Publications*.

Simon De Deyne, Amy Perfors, and Daniel J Navarro. 2016. Predicting human similarity judgments with distributional models: The value of word associations. In *Proceedings of COLING*.

William Dyer. 2018. Integration complexity and the order of cosisters. In *Proceedings of the Second Workshop on Universal Dependencies (UDW 2018)*, pages 55–65.

Victor S. Ferreira and Carla E Firato. 2002. Proactive interference effects on sentence production. *Psychonomic bulletin review*, 9(2):795 – 800.

V.S. Ferreira and G.S. Dell. 2000. Effect of Ambiguity and Lexical Availability on Syntactic and Lexical Production* 1. *Cognitive Psychology*, 40(4):296–340.

Richard Futrell. 2019. Information-theoretic locality properties of natural language. In *Proceedings of the First Workshop on Quantitative Syntax (Quasy, SyntaxFest 2019)*.

Richard Futrell, William Dyer, and Gregory Scontras. 2020a. What determines the order of adjectives in english? comparing efficiency-based theories using dependency corpora. In *Proceedings of ACL 2020*.

Richard Futrell, Edward Gibson, and Roger P. Levy. 2020b. Lossy-context surprisal: An information-theoretic model of memory effects in sentence processing. *Cognitive Science*, 44:e12814.

Richard Futrell, Roger P. Levy, and Edward Gibson. 2020c. Dependency locality as an explanatory principle for word order. *Language*, 96(2):371–413.

Richard Futrell, Peng Qian, Edward Gibson, Evelina Fedorenko, and Idan Blank. 2019. Syntactic dependencies correspond to word pairs with high mutual information. In *Proceedings of the Fifth International Conference on Dependency Linguistics*.

Silvia P. Gennari, Jelena Mirković, and Maryellen C. MacDonald. 2012. Animacy and competition in relative clause production: A cross-linguistic investigation. *Cognitive Psychology*, 65(2):141 – 176.

Edward Gibson, Richard Futrell, Steven T. Piantadosi, Isabelle Dautriche, Kyle Mahowald, Leon Bergen, and Roger Levy. 2019. How efficiency shapes human language. *Trends in Cognitive Sciences*.

Peter C. Gordon, Randall Hendrick, Marcus Johnson, and Yoonhyoung Lee. 2006. Similarity-based interference during language comprehension: Evidence from eye tracking during reading. *Journal of Experimental Psychology: Learning, Memory, and Cognition*, 32(6):1304–1321.

Edouard Grave, Piotr Bojanowski, Prakhar Gupta, Armand Joulin, and Tomas Mikolov. 2018. Learning word vectors for 157 languages. In *Proceedings of the LREC 2018*.

Thomas L Griffiths, Mark Steyvers, and Joshua B Tenenbaum. 2007. Topics in semantic representation. *Psychological review*, 114(2):211.

John T. Hale. 2001. A probabilistic Earley parser as a psycholinguistic model. In *Proceedings of the Second Meeting of the NAACL*, pages 1–8.

John A. Hawkins. 2014. *Cross-linguistic variation and efficiency*. Oxford University Press, Oxford.

Gina F. Humphreys, Jelena Mirković, and Silvia P. Gennari. 2016. Similarity-based competition in relative clause production and comprehension. *Journal of Memory and Language*, 89:200 – 221. Speaking and Listening: Relationships Between Language Production and Comprehension.

Samar Husain, Rajesh Bhatt, and Shravan Vasishth. 2013. Towards a psycholinguistically motivated dependency grammar for Hindi. In *Proceedings of the Second International Conference on Dependency Linguistics (DepLing 2013)*, pages 108–117.

Samar Husain, Shravan Vasishth, and Narayanan Srinivasan. 2014. Strong expectations cancel locality effects: Evidence from Hindi. *PLOS ONE*, 9(7):e100986.

T. Florian Jaeger. 2010. Redundancy and reduction: Speakers manage syntactic information density. *Cognitive Psychology*, 61(1):23–62.

T. Florian Jaeger and Harry J. Tily. 2011. On language 'utility': Processing complexity and communicative efficiency. *Wiley Interdisciplinary Reviews: Cognitive Science*, 2(3):323–335.

Lena Jäger, Felix Engelmann, and Shravan Vasishth. 2017. Similarity-based interference in sentence comprehension: Literature review and Bayesian meta-analysis. *Journal of Memory and Language*, 94:316–339.

Ayush Jain, Vishal Singh, Sidharth Ranjan, Rajakrishnan Rajkumar, and Sumeet Agarwal. 2018. Uniform information density effects on syntactic choice in Hindi. In *Proceedings of the Workshop on Linguistic Complexity and Natural Language Processing*.

Itisree Jena, Riyaz Ahmad Bhat, Sambhav Jain, and Dipti Misra Sharma. 2013. Animacy annotation in the Hindi treebank. In *Proceedings of the 7th Linguistic Annotation Workshop and Interoperability with Discourse*.

Lars Konieczny. 2000. Locality and parsing complexity. *Journal of Psycholinguistic Research*, 29(6):627–645.

Anoop Kunchukuttan, Pratik Mehta, and Pushpak Bhattacharyya. 2017. The iit bombay english-hindi parallel corpus. *arXiv preprint arXiv:1710.02855*.

Chigusa Kurumada and T. Florian Jaeger. 2015. Communicative efficiency in language production: Optional case-marking in japanese. *Journal of Memory and Language*, 83:152 – 178.

Richard L Lewis and Mineharu Nakayama. 2002. Syntactic and positional similarity effects in the processing of japanese embeddings. *Sentence processing in East Asian languages*, pages 85–110.

Richard L. Lewis and Shravan Vasishth. 2005. An activation-based model of sentence processing as skilled memory retrieval. *Cognitive Science*, 29(3):375–419.

Haitao Liu, Chunshan Xu, and Junying Liang. 2017. Dependency distance: A new perspective on syntactic patterns in natural languages. *Physics of Life Reviews*, 21:171–193.

Maryellen C. MacDonald. 2013. How language production shapes language form and comprehension. *Frontiers in Psychology*, 4:226.

Paola Merlo and Francesco Ackermann. 2018. Vectorial semantic spaces do not encode human judgments of intervention similarity. In *Proceedings of the 22nd CoNLL*, pages 392–401.

Shota Momma and Victor S. Ferreira. 2019. Beyond linear order: The role of argument structure in speaking. *Cognitive Psychology*, 114:101228.

Emily Morgan and Roger Levy. 2016. Abstract knowledge versus direct experience in processing of binomial expressions. *Cognition*, 157:382–402.

Joakim Nivre. 2008. Algorithms for deterministic incremental dependency parsing. *Computational Linguistics*, 34(4):513–553.

Liam Paninski. 2003. Estimation of entropy and mutual information. *Neural Computation*, 15(6):1191–1253.

Mercè Prat-Sala and Holly P Branigan. 2000. Discourse constraints on syntactic processing in language production: A cross-linguistic study in english and spanish. *Journal of Memory and Language*, 42(2):168 – 182.

Sidharth Ranjan, Sumeet Agarwal, and Rajakrishnan Rajkumar. 2019. Surprisal and interference effects of case markers in Hindi word order. In *Proceedings of the Workshop on Cognitive Modeling and Computational Linguistics*, pages 30–42.

Gerard Salton. 1972. A new comparison between conventional indexing (medlars) and automatic text processing (smart). *Journal of the American Society for Information Science*, 23(2):75–84.

Kartik Sharma, Kaivalya Swami, Aditya Shete, and Samar Husain. 2019. Can Greenbergian universals be induced from language networks? In *Proceedings of the 18th International Workshop on Treebanks and Linguistic Theories*.

Garrett Smith and Shravan Vasishth. 2020. A principled approach to feature selection in models ofsentence processing.

David Temperley and Daniel Gildea. 2018. Minimizing syntactic dependency lengths: Typological/cognitive universal? *Annual Review of Linguistics*, 4:1–15.

Shravan Vasishth. 2003. *Working memory in sentence comprehension: Processing Hindi center embeddings*. Routledge.

Shravan Vasishth. 2004. Discourse Context and Word Order Preferences in Hindi. In *R. Singh (ed.), The Yearbook of South Asian Languages and Linguistics*, pages 113–127.

Shravan Vasishth and Samar Husain. 2014. The interaction of working memory and expectation-based processes in sentence comprehension. In *Technical report of IEICE. Thought and language*, volume 114(176), pages 113–114.

Himanshu Yadav, Ashwini Vaidya, Vishakha Shukla, and Samar Husain. 2020. Word order typology interacts with linguistic complexity: a cross-linguistic corpus study. *Cognitive Science*, (44).

George Kingsley Zipf. 1949. *Human behavior and the principle of least effort*. Addison-Wesley Press, Oxford, UK.

Images and Imagination: Automated Analysis of Priming Effects Related to Autism Spectrum Disorder and Developmental Language Disorder

Michaela Regneri[1]
OTTO (GmbH & Co. KG)
Hamburg, Germany
regneri@googlemail.com

Diane King
The Open University
Milton Keynes, United Kingdom
d.king@open.ac.uk

Fahreen Walji[1]
University of Roehampton
London, United Kingdom

Olympia Palikara
University of Warwick
Coventry, United Kingdom
Olympia.Palikara@warwick.ac.uk

Abstract

Different aspects of language processing have been shown to be sensitive to priming but the findings of studies examining priming effects in adolescents with Autism Spectrum Disorder (ASD) and Developmental Language Disorder (DLD) have been inconclusive. We present a study analysing visual and implicit semantic priming in adolescents with ASD and DLD. Based on a dataset of fictional and script-like narratives, we evaluate how often and how extensively, content of two different priming sources is used by the participants. The first priming source was visual, consisting of images shown to the participants to assist them with their storytelling. The second priming source originated from commonsense knowledge, using crowdsourced data containing prototypical script elements. Our results show that individuals with ASD are less sensitive to both types of priming, but show typical usage of primed cues when they use them at all. In contrast, children with DLD show mostly average priming sensitivity, but exhibit an over-proportional use of the priming cues.

1 Introduction

This study compares the effects of priming on the narratives of adolescents with Autism Spectrum Disorder with those of adolescents with Developmental Language Disorders[2]. Priming occurs when exposure to one stimulus influences the response to a subsequent stimulus. This is an unconscious process whereby an association is activated in memory just before a new stimulus is seen or a task is introduced and is thought to play an important role in facilitating language fluency (MacDonald,

2013), implicit language learning (Dell and Chang, 2014), and in conversation and social interaction (e.g. Bresnan et al., 2007). Different aspects of language processing have been shown to be sensitive to priming (KIDD, 2012; Rämä et al., 2013) but whilst studies have typically examined priming effects in children (Foltz et al., 2015; Goldwater et al., 2011), there is a paucity of literature comparing priming effects in adolescents with ASD with those of adolescents with DLD.

Both ASD and DLD are communication disorders, with individuals in these clinical groups often having overlapping language phenotypes (Tomblin, 2011). However, it is unclear whether or not the language difficulties they exhibit have the same or different underlying aetiology (Manolitsi and Botting, 2011). ASD is a neurodevelopmental disorder characterised by impairments in social interaction, verbal and nonverbal communication and restricted and repetitive behaviours (APA, 2013). DLDs affect about 7.5% of children during their first year of school (Norbury and Bishop, 2003; Tomblin, 2011), and are associated with different language difficulties (e.g phonology, semantics and syntax). These impairments can be receptive, expressive or mixed (APA, 2013) and are likely to persist into adolescence and young adulthood (Conti-Ramsden and Botting, 1999; Dockrell et al., 2007).

Research has shown that both individuals with ASD and those with DLD produce narratives that are impoverished in comparison to their typically developing peers, displaying difficulties in both macrostructure and microstructure (Wetherell et al., 2007; Rezzonico et al., 2015; King et al., 2013, 2014). Studies comparing narratives of children from these two clinical groups have found few differences in structural language, evaluation and pragmatic measures (Norbury and Bishop, 2003; Manolitsi and Botting, 2011; Frazier Norbury et al., 2013). As yet, it is not clear if this is because both

---

[1]The first and third authors conducted this research independently, this paper is not related to their current affiliations.

[2]Following recent recommendations (Bishop et al., 2016, 2017), the term Developmental Language Disorders has been adopted and used throughout in this paper.

Proceedings of the Workshop on Cognitive Modeling and Computational Linguistics, pages 11–27
Online Event, November 19, 2020. ©2020 Association for Computational Linguistics
https://doi.org/10.18653/v1/P17

groups have the same underlying language difficulties, or if there are diagnostic specific factors affecting their narrative production.

Narrative difficulties of individuals with ASD may be explained, in part, by the information processing theory of weak central coherence. This theory proposes that something within the typical cognitive system derives meaning by relating incoming information to global context (Frith, 1989; Happe and Frith, 2006). Frith argued that individuals with ASD display differences to neurotypicals in this aspect of information processing, resulting in a tendency to focus on details at the expense of the whole. It is possible that the ability to make use of context to infer meaning is related to priming effects in language. If this is so, then we would expect individuals with ASD to display differences in priming compared to both their typically developing peers and the DLD group which would be reflected in their narrative language.

There is clearly a need for further research in this area and, to date, we can find none that compares priming effects in individuals with an ASD or DLD. We believe this to be an important area to explore for a number of reasons. A better understanding of the specific areas of difficulty experienced by both these clinical groups in not only structural, but also other forms of priming would inform the planning of appropriate intervention and support. Furthermore, if differences in priming are found between the two groups, this may give some indication as to whether or not the language difficulties they exhibit arise from the same or different underlying aetiology. Moreover, if individuals with ASD, but not those with DLD, display difficulties in priming, this may offer support for the theory of weak central coherence as an explanation for autism. In this study, our aim was to investigate priming effects in language production at the discourse level in adolescents with these communication disorders. In order to do so, we analysed visual and script based priming cues, and the extent to which these types of context present difficulties for individuals with ASD or DLD. A further aim was to examine whether these effects are related to language competency and development, or originated from typical traits of individuals with ASD.

This paper is structured as follows: After a review of related work (Sec. 2), we describe the dataset (Sec. 3) underlying our experiments (Sec. 4). After a discussion of the results (Sec. 5)

we conclude with a short summary and suggestions for future research (Sec. 6).

2   Related Work

To date, research into priming effects on the language of individuals with either ASD or DLD, has primarily focused on structural or syntactic priming. The findings are inconclusive, but suggest that both these groups exhibit less ability to benefit from priming cues than typically developing children (Kamio et al., 2007). Mottron et al. (2001) have shown that individuals with ASD benefit more from phonological cues than semantic cues. Evidence from fMRI scans also suggests that the performance of individuals may depend on perceptual rather than semantic processing (Gaffrey et al., 2007). Hala et al. (2007) showed that for children with ASD, priming cues are rarely sufficient to change previously triggered meanings of homographs.

Studies of priming in individuals with DLD are similarly inconclusive. Miller and Deevy (2006) found that children with DLD displayed similar syntactic priming effects as typically developing children. However, another study using a structural priming paradigm (Garraffa et al., 2015) suggests that children with DLD show a smaller cumulative priming effect. Garraffa et al. (2018) later concluded that children with DLD exhibit patterns of syntactic priming effects which are consistent with an impairment in implicit learning mechanisms. In this experiment, none of the groups showed a significant cumulative priming effect.

Our investigation of priming effects required suitable raw data together with either extensive manual annotation or adequate computational methods. We decided to apply methods from the field of computational stylometry, which is concerned with the analysis of (written or transcribed) text and how it reveals information about the person who has produced this (Daelemans, 2013).

For DLD, there are virtually no approaches to automated analyses: Gabani et al. (2009, 2011) detected language impairment in Spanish texts, with a focus on the classification task itself rather than on stylometric analyses of explaining features.

There are, however, some studies where language difficulties typical in ASD have been subject to automated analysis. Most approaches have tried to automatically classify texts by individuals with ASD: Prud'hommeaux et al. (2011) built an automated classifier for sentences uttered by very young children (6-7 years old), distinguishing between an ASD group and two comparison groups (one with children with a language impairment, one with typically developing children). The authors themselves note some drawbacks of their underlying dataset, in particular that some children in the ASD group were also classified as language-impaired. Consequently, it was not possible to demonstrate a clear distinction between the groups.

In two follow-up studies (Rouhizadeh et al., 2013, 2015), the authors analysed whole narratives (retellings) of children (mean age 6.4) with ASD compared to a typically developing comparison group. The texts from the comparison group and some crowdsourced retellings from typically developing adults served as a basis for determining unusualness. We adopted parts of this idea and, in our study, collected data via crowdsourcing and matched it to the narratives under research. In our case, the collected data does not consist of whole narratives, but rather abstract prototypical facts.

Beyond the classification approaches, De Bruyne et al. (2018) present a detailed feature analysis of Dutch texts by adolescents with ASD, identifying shallow and deep features that indicate ASD-related difficulties. Our own work (Regneri and King, 2015, 2016) also reports different shallow and discourse-based analyses of stories by children with ASD, compared to two control groups. We have used the same data source and have taken these analyses a step further. Moving beyond text-based analyses, we have targeted contextual priming effects. In addition to examining language typical for ASD, we have extended the dataset and also evaluated texts by adolescents with DLD.

3 Datasets

Our analysis was based on datasets by King et al. (2013, 2014) and by King and Palikara (2018a). The corpus contains transcripts of two types of stories: *fictional* stories and stories we call *event* narratives which describe common scenarios. Following is a description of the participant groups, the two story types and a short summary of the whole corpus.

3.1 Participants and Experimental Setup

The first cohort of participants comprised three groups: 27 high functioning adolescents with ASD (11 to 14 years old), one comparison group of 27 adolescents matched with the ASD group on chronological age and nonverbal ability ("age-matched" peers, AM), and a second comparison group of 27 adolescents (7 to 14 years old), who were individually matched with the ASD group on a measure of expressive language (Recalling Sentences subtest of the CELF IV (Semel et al., 2006)) and on nonverbal ability ("language-matched" peers, LM). All groups had average scores on non-verbal and verbal measures, as measured by the Matrices test of the BAS II (Elliot et al., 1996) and the BPVS II (Dunn and Dunn, 1997). There were no significant differences between the groups in measures of non-verbal ability, verbal ability or expressive language. The average age difference between the language-matched comparison group and the two other groups was 17 months. This dataset was extended by King and Palikara (2018b) with data from 25 adolescents with DLD, who were matched to the ASD group by age and non-verbal but not verbal ability. Children with Developmental Language Disorder often experience vocabulary difficulties and delays when compared to their typically developing peers (Gray et al., 1999; Rice et al., 2010; Rice and Hoffman, 2015). The profile of the children with DLD in this study on the BPVS is very much in line with that reported by other studies in the field, highlighting the deficits these children experience in receptive vocabulary when compared to other groups of children. See Table 1 for some basic characteristics of the three groups.

For data collection, each participant generated two fictional narratives and 12 different event narratives. The participants constructed these narratives following different prompts, accompanied with a supporting picture. In the experimental setup, fictional and event narratives were elicited in turn, with 6 event narratives followed by a fictional narrative. In our experiments, we used both the accompanying images and the script-like event scenarios as priming sources. The Appendix shows the instructions given to the participants, examples from the story collection and the image stimuli.

3.2 Fictional Narratives

For the fictional dataset, King et al. (2014) presented participants in all four groups with the following two story stems, along with a drawing, and asked them to continue the narrative:

1. The "forest" story: *The boy ran into the forest.*

Group	ASD	DLD	LM	AM
Participants	27	26	27	27
Age in years	12.77	12.44	11.33	12.77
SD	(0.96)	(1.56)	(2.96)	(0.82)
BPVS II score	104.50	75.19	110.93	107.14
SD	(20.97)	(12.77)	(13.22)	(15.36)

Table 1: Mean age and test scores of ASD, DLD, Language Match (LM) and Age Match Group (AM). Standard deviation (SD) is shown in brackets.

	words / text			words / utterance		
	GEN	SEN	FIC	GEN	SEN	FIC
ASD	191	244	162	6.6	7.2	14.4
DLD	209	218	182	5.9	7.0	14.1
LM	252	400	220	10.5	10.2	16.9
AM	280	420	182	11.8	11.0	17.2

Table 2: Text and utterance length of all narratives, by comparison group and narrative types.

> *He looked ahead of him and saw a little green man in a spaceship.*

2. The "mountain" story: *When the girl climbed up the mountain, she saw, hidden among the trees, a little wooden house covered in snow.*

King et al. (2014) recorded the stories, transcribed, manually coded and scored them according to the Narrative Scoring Scheme (Stein and Albro, 1997).

3.3 Event Narratives

The corpus of event narratives (King et al., 2013) contains transcripts of short stories, describing one of 6 everyday scenarios each: SPENDING FREE TIME, BEING ANGRY WITH SOMEBODY, GOING ON HOLIDAYS, HAVING A BIRTHDAY, HALLOWEEN and BEING SCARED.

Every participant told two narratives for each of the scenarios: first a *specific narrative* (SEN) about a particular instance (answering a prompt like "Can you tell me about a time when you went on holiday?"), and second a *general narrative* (GEN) that contains a script-like prototypical scenario description ("What usually happens when someone goes on holiday?"). Overall, the set contains 1272 narratives (2×6 stories per participant).

Table 2 presents basic statistics for the whole corpus. The figures distinguish the participant groups and additionally the fictional (FIC) narratives from the general (GEN) and specific (SEN) event narratives. The narratives from the ASD and the DLD group were, in general, shorter than those of the

comparison groups, both with respect to the overall story length and the mean length of utterance.

3.4 Contextual and Visual Priming

The dataset allowed us to differentiate between issues of language development and ASD-specific difficulties, because it has two control groups matched accordingly. Content-wise, the stories enable research on specific priming effects in ASD and DLD, namely *image-based* priming, cued by visual situational context, and *script-based* priming, reflecting the influence of prototypical structures. Our study evaluated whether and how often both types of content appear in the narratives.

As a source for image-based priming, the corpus contains pictures used to support the adolescents' story telling. Our second source for priming was scripts: Scripts (Schank and Abelson, 1977) are pieces of commonsense knowledge describing everyday scenarios (e.g. *going to a restaurant*). They contain events (*ordering, eating,...*) and their participants (*food, waiter, ...*). Script-based priming means that a prototypical event representation is evoked and influences the story contents. To investigate related priming effects, we studied how much prototypical content is reflected in the adolescents' (specific) event narratives, and then related this to their overall ability to describe the prototypical scenarios (in the general event narratives).

4 Priming Experiments

We examined scripts and images as two different priming sources, and analysed the influence of these different contextual cues in narrations by adolescents with ASD, DLD and neurotypical developing peers. We thus distinguished the priming mechanisms that reflect the developmental stage of language competency (by comparing the language-matched group with the ASD group), fundamental differences in language development (comparing the DLD group with the other groups) or typical traits of individuals with ASD.

We will first present our definition of priming and the goals of our experiments (4.1). After describing how we crowdsourced textual representations of the different priming stimuli (4.2) and which measures we used to relate them to the narratives (4.3), we outline the results (4.4)

4.1 Priming from Images and Scripts

Our experiments evaluated different aspects of priming. We used priming in a slightly unusual sense here, referring to the reflection of cues in the generation of narratives. The cues we examined were both nonlinguistic cues, originating from two different types of context.

4.1.1 Visual priming from images

We defined *visual priming* as the extent to which an image-based cue is reflected in a narrative that does not describe the image itself. In this study, participants were presented with pictures to support the construction of their narratives, but these might or might not be used for this purpose. Our focus was to evaluate to what degree this visual context affected the narratives produced by each group. We hypothesised that if the narratives of a specific group contained a large proportion of references to the image, this would indicate a heavy reliance on the picture as support. This suggests that they may be experiencing difficulties in constructing narratives independently and may indicate the presence of a developmental language disorder. On the other hand, if very little or no visual context is verbalised, we can infer that participants are having difficulties either processing or applying information from the images. It is of course also possible, that they simply choose not to use this information.

4.1.2 Contextual priming from scripts

Contextual priming is what we find if a certain situational context is evoked by a story scenario, and different aspects of this context are evident in the narrative. This is related to both the linguistic theory of scripts, and the linguistic and socio-psychological theories of framing and frame semantics (Fillmore, 1976; Goffman, 1979). Using common sense scenarios as priming sources means that we do not evaluate the effects of specific cues (like images). What we did instead was to measure how easily such a prototypical context is evoked, and how much of the narrative content is derived directly from this context.

Our hypotheses are the same as they are for visual priming. Narratives that show a high proportion of script-based context indicate the ability to evoke the respective script, but also point to potential deficits in thinking of narrative elements outside the primed scenario. Alternatively, should the narratives of one of the clinical groups show no use of script-based context, this would suggest difficulties in the application of shared common-sense knowledge, a feature associated with ASD.

4.2 Experimental Priming Data

We needed additional data to examine the two different types of priming: For *image-based* priming, we collected descriptions of the images shown together with the story prompt. In order to compare this with *script-based priming*, we also collected entities prototypically associated with the given scenarios. Previous research has argued that script data is hard to obtain from standard texts or word embeddings (Regneri et al., 2010), so we decided to use crowdsourcing for both types of data.

Using Amazon Mechanical Turk (AMT), we set up two separate experiments. We collected Image descriptions by presenting the drawings and asking participants for one-word descriptions of the images' contents, encouraging them to name visible entities as well as associated events or moods. For each image, we asked 10 distinct turkers to provide at least 2 and at most 10 words. The participants did not see any verbal description of the picture.

In a similar fashion, we also crowdsourced prototypical script data: For each scenario (both fictional and event-based), we asked which things, people or actions the turkers would typically expect when the given event occurs. We explicitly noted that some scenarios might be fictional and advised the participants to name things they would expect in a story featuring the given scenario. The images were not shown to the participants.

After manually filtering out obvious fraughts, incomprehensible inputs and inputs neglecting the task (15% overall), we aggregated the data and kept all descriptions that occurred at least twice. We have provided the collected data and the image stimuli in the appendix and as supplementary data.

Table 3 contains some basic figures on the preprocessed data, including the number of words retained for both tasks and the overlap of both lemma sets (as Jaccard score). The overlap between image-based data and script data indicates prototypicalness: scenarios represented by a more concise inventory of entities show a higher overlap between descriptions derived from pictures and from commonsense scenarios.

4.3 Measures

After obtaining textual representations of the priming cues, we related these to our narratives. Technically, we measured the overlap of the AMT data

Scenario	Image	Script	Jaccard
FOREST	6	4	0.25
MOUNTAIN	12	7	0.19
FREE TIME	21	10	0.15
BE SCARED	16	12	0.00
BIRTHDAY	9	11	0.11
HOLIDAY	18	8	0.04
HALLOWEEN	11	7	0.06
BE ANGRY	10	7	0.06

Table 3: Statistics on crowdsourced priming data, showing the number of words for the two experiments and their overlap measured as Jaccard index.

with the story vocabulary. Considered in isolation, a low overlap is not indicative, because various reasons could explain the absence of crowdsourced vocabulary in the stories (differences in task, age, nationalities, and so on). We did assume, however, that comparing the presence of such vocabulary can positively indicate whether or not the participants do incorporate extra-linguistic context into their stories, and how the groups differ in doing so.

We measured two types of overlap: first we counted how many stories contained any of the primed expressions at all (*stories primed*):

$$\text{stories}_{pr} = \frac{|\{\text{ stories w. AMT vocabulary}\}|}{|\{\text{all stories}\}|}$$

While this indicated the *general prevalence* of priming in the participants, we also evaluated the *usage of priming-based vocabulary*, measuring how many content words of a story s consisted of priming-based data (*vocab primed*) as follows:

$$\text{vocab}_{pr}(s) = \frac{|\{\text{content words in s} \cap \text{AMT data}\}|}{|\{\text{all content words in s}\}|}$$

We defined content words to be all nouns, verbs, adjectives and adverbs, according to POS tagging with CoreNLP (Manning et al., 2014). The extreme cases are that either no content word has a priming source ($\text{vocab}_{pr}(s) = 0$), or that there is no word without a priming source ($\text{vocab}_{pr}(s) = 1$, e.g. two words describing the picture). For our evaluation, we calculate $\oslash\text{vocab}_{pr}$ as the average primed vocabulary over all stories s.

Differences in priming effects between the groups were examined using a χ^2-test for stories_{pr} and an independent samples t test for vocab_{pr}. As the analysis of the scores necessitated the use of multiple tests, in order to control for a type 1 error, we adopted a more stringent α-level, $p < 0.01$.

Stimulus type	ASD	DLD	LM	AM
Images	0.54	0.58	0.70	0.73
Scripts	0.59	0.63	0.69	0.67

Table 4: Overall proportion of stories primed.

Group	type	stories_{pr}	$\oslash$ vocab_{pr} (SD)
ASD	GEN	0.61	0.09 (0.12)
	SEN	**0.39**	0.05 (0.10)
	FIC	**0.76**	0.07 (0.06)
DLD	GEN	**0.56**	0.09 (0.15)
	SEN	0.49	**0.07** (0.12)
	FIC	0.90	0.08 (0.06)
LM	GEN	0.72	0.09 (0.10)
	SEN	0.60	0.05 (0.07)
	FIC	0.92	0.07 (0.05)
AM	GEN	0.77	0.08 (0.09)
	SEN	0.63	0.05 (0.08)
	FIC	0.91	0.06 (0.03)

Table 5: The percentage of stories with image-based content and the average proportion of priming-based vocabulary per story, divided by story type.

4.4 Results

Table 4 displays the overall results for the script-based and the image-based experiment, indicating the proportion of stories primed. Overall, the ASD group exhibited the lowest priming effects. In the image-based experiment, both the ASD and the DLD groups differ significantly from the two control groups, but not from each other. For the script-based condition, the ASD group narrates significantly fewer primed stories than the language-matched group and notably fewer than the age-matched group ($p < 0.02$), while the other three groups show no significant difference in this scenario. While it seems that the ASD and the DLD groups only differ for script-based priming, a more detailed examination of the data allows for a more informative differentiation.

4.5 Image-based Priming

Table 5 distinguishes the story types and additionally shows the proportion of primed vocabulary. In their fictional stories, the ASD group displayed a significantly lower proportion of primed stories than the other groups, while the proportion of priming based vocabulary does not differ from the control groups. The average use of priming based vocabulary ($\oslash$ vocab_{pr}) was higher in the DLD group ($p < 0.05$), but there were no significant differences between any of the other groups. Note that the proportion of vocabulary also includes stories without any primed content, so this figure implicitly reflects the proportion of primed stories.

As expected, we find less primed vocabulary in the event narratives: Firstly, the fictional story pictures contained some elements mentioned by nearly all participants (like the alien), showing that the adolescents took this picture as a starting point rather than an optional support. Secondly, the specific event narratives contained stories from the participants' personal histories, for which we expected a smaller priming effect. Most groups indeed distinguished clearly between general and specific narratives. While the stories as a whole contained prototypical concepts in both cases, the proportion of vocabulary originating from priming sources showed an interesting trend: the general narratives contained a similar amount of vocabulary from priming sources in all groups and the specific narratives for the DLD group contained a larger amount than those of all other groups (the difference between GEN and SEN is not significant, while it is significant for all other groups).

These more detailed figures present a different perspective on the number of stories primed: While the average number primed was very similar in both the ASD and the DLD groups and much lower than in the control groups, the ASD group showed a clear distinction between general and specific narratives, and a lower priming sensitivity on average. The DLD group had the same priming sensitivity for the fictional stories we find for the AM and the LM groups, but showed comparable priming effects for specific and general contexts.

As far as the proportion of primed vocabulary is concerned, additional invention of vocabulary (concepts not shown in the picture) for the specific narratives is triggered for the ASD, AM and LM groups but not the DLD group. While on average, the ASD group used priming-based vocabulary in fewer cases than all other groups, the vocabulary was used in an unmarked way if used at all. The DLD group, however, while showing a typical frequency of priming effects, built their specific stories more on the primed concepts than the other groups. For the general event narratives, the DLD group shows less priming sensitivity than any other group, underlining the unusual similarity of the two event variants (GEN and SEN).

Group	type	% stories	⊘ vocab (SD)
ASD	GEN	0.70	0.11 (0.12)
	SEN	**0.45**	0.05 (0.10)
	FIC	**0.66**	0.05 (0.06)
DLD	GEN	**0.66**	0.11 (0.14)
	SEN	0.58	**0.08** (0.10)
	FIC	0.73	0.05 (0.05)
LM	GEN	0.73	0.10 (0.09)
	SEN	0.63	0.06 (0.07)
	FIC	0.76	0.04 (0.04)
AM	GEN	0.73	0.09 (0.08)
	SEN	0.63	0.05 (0.07)
	FIC	0.76	0.04 (0.03)

Table 6: The percentage of stories with script-based content and the average proportion of priming-based vocabulary per story, divided by story type.

4.6 Script-based Priming

Table 6 summarises the results for script-based priming. None of the groups differed significantly in the fictional stories. This was to some degree expected: while there are some prototypical associations with "alien scenarios" of "snowy secluded mountain scenarios", these fictional contexts do not give rise to actual scripts in the sense of prototypical everyday actions. In the event narratives, the average proportion of stories containing contextually primed content was significantly lower in the ASD group than in both of the comparison groups (LM $p < 0.01$, AM $p < 0.05$), while the DLD group does not differ significantly from any group.

Similar to the image-based experiment, both the use of script-based vocabulary and the distinction between the general and specific narratives seems to be related to language competency rather than to ASD (cf. Table 6): While all other groups showed significant differences between general and specific narratives ($p < 0.01$), the DLD group showed the least ($p = 0.02$). Comparing the proportions of vocabulary used, the DLD group showed a higher proportion of priming-based vocabulary than the two comparison groups both on average and in the specific event setting ($p < 0.01$).

Both the percentage of narratives with primed content and the proportion of vocabulary from priming cues was, in general, higher for script-based priming, even in the fictional narratives. For event narratives, this is due to the nature of general narratives, which contain a prototypical scenario description and thus reflect exactly what we used as priming cues. Relating them to the crowdsourced data analyzes, therefore, not actual priming but rather an alignment with concepts from the same scenario. Script-based priming is reflected better in the specific narratives, which contain personal narrations of individual events. Here the average priming level resembles the image-based priming results.

5   Results and Discussion

In this section, we interpret our results and review to what extent they answer open questions about priming in adolescents with ASD and with DLD.

5.1   Priming effects in ASD and DLD

We compared script-based and visual priming, and the results show notable differences between the groups. On average, the ASD group uses priming cues less frequently than all other groups. This is particularly evident for script-based priming, where the ASD group shows fewer average priming effects than both of the comparison groups, in contrast to the DLD group whose intermediate priming frequency does not differ significantly from any other group (cf. Table 4).

These results indicate either a lack of, or an inability to apply, script-based abstract knowledge, as a typical trait of the ASD group. As it is not evident in either the language-matched group or the group with manifested language development disorder, the script-related phenomena are independent of language ability. Our data suggests that the ASD group can probably access the scripts per se - this is supported by their unmarked priming sensitivity for general narratives. However, they relate their personal stories to the underlying script less frequently than the other groups, which suggests an inability to connect specific content to a broader context. At the same time, the partially low priming sensitivity of the DLD group might simply be a correlate of smaller or atypical vocabulary.

With regard to the extent of which cue-based concepts are used, participants with ASD do not differ from the neurotypical comparison groups: primed content is present in the same proportion of vocabulary. Further, the ASD group and the two comparison groups differentiate between general and specific event narratives in the same way, with more priming cues reflected in the former and fewer in the latter. However, unlike the ASD group, individuals with DLD show a lack of differentiation between general scenario descriptions and specific narratives. Compared to the ASD group, they use fewer priming cues in the general narratives, but they do so more often in the specific case. This means that the overall effect appears similar to the ASD group, but suggests that there may be different underlying causes. Their narratives also contain more cued content than the comparison groups.

Our findings concerning image-based priming complement previous research on language understanding: Yaneva et al. (2015) showed that adults with autism profit more than neurotypical controls from supporting images for text comprehension. In contrast, our study, found that supporting images contributed more rarely to the narrative stories of the ASD group than in all of the neurotypical groups. However, there are important differences between the studies in terms of the age of the participants and the matching of control groups. Not withstanding, the distinction between priming for language understanding and language production remains an interesting area to explore further.

5.2   Implications and Open Questions

Our results further the understanding of the use of context in narrative construction. The ASD group makes less use of context in their narratives than all other groups. However, when they do use context, they do so in a typical manner. This is in contrast to the DLD group. While this group also uses context less frequently than the comparison groups, context use is over-proportional when they do so, especially in unexpected cases as in the narratives with personal experiences. These results support previous findings showing that children with ASD demonstrate impairment in priming, but no absolute inability to use contextual information (Henderson et al., 2011). Moreover, they lend support to the theory of weak central coherence which proposes that individuals with ASD have difficulties in processing incoming information in context for global meaning. In contrast, the DLD group shows slightly lower priming sensitivity than the comparison groups, but when they do so, their use of primed content is over-proportional, especially in the specific event narratives.

The indications are that this impairment in priming is independent of language ability and specific to ASD. The DLD group shows a different pattern of impairment, indicating a different underlying aetiology than in the ASD group. The over-proportional use of context by the DLD group might be a compensation for their difficulties in language production.

This study delivers only some initial indicators of priming in individuals with ASD and DLD and it has a number of limitations. Firstly, this is not a classical priming study because we are examining language production rather than comprehension, and we have analysed content at the discourse-level rather than word selection or sentential structures. Given this complex task, we employed a simple pragmatic approach for initial analysis. We are aware that our results cannot give a precise account of the extent or nature of priming effects on a discourse level, but this was not the aim of the study. Rather, we targeted a comparative view of different groups, showing how explicit (visual) and implicit (script-based) cues influence the narration style of differently developing adolescents.

The evidence we have found suggests a division of these priming effects which can be either attributed to autism spectrum disorder, or developmental language disorder, or neither of these communication disorders. While this is not theory-sound proof of either attribution so far, we have developed some data-informed hypotheses as a source for new questions and further experiments.

6 Conclusion

We conclude this paper with a short summary and some suggestions for future work.

6.1 Summary

Our study evaluated visual and script-based priming effects in individuals with ASD and DLD, in comparison to neurotypical control groups. We based our analyses on a dataset containing fictional and event-based narratives of adolescents with ASD, DLD and two age-matched and language-matched comparison groups. Additionally, we crowdsourced textual representations of images and scenario descriptions as priming cues. In our experiment, we demonstrated the overlap of these representations with the narratives in our dataset and differentiated the text types for the different groups. Our findings show that, although in general less sensitive to priming cues, adolescents with ASD use these cues either not at all or in the same way as neurotypical peers. In contrast, adolescents with DLD show a typical sensitivity to priming cues in most cases, but exhibit an overproportional use of primed content.

6.2 Future Work

To the best of our knowledge, there is no preceding work showing priming effects on language production in adolescents with ASD or DLD. While we have found interesting initial results, there are still many unanswered questions. Further research is needed to test if these findings are replicable. Future work could examine other aspects of priming, in particular differences in priming in all groups between scripts and images.

Future experiments could observe participants' attention while relating the narratives, which would give real-time indications of a priming mechanism. More data containing both different languages and offering other sources of extra-linguistic priming would help to explore the circumstances that facilitate or inhibit priming effects in individuals with ASD. With regards to priming effects in adolescents with DLD, analysing their capability to distinguish between general and specific event narratives could also be fruitful area of research.

References

APA. 2013. *Diagnostic and statistical manual of mental disorders: DSM-5*, 5th ed. edition. American Psychiatric Association, Washington, DC.

Dorothy V.M. Bishop, Margaret J. Snowling, Paul A. Thompson, Trisha Greenhalgh, , and the CATALISE-2 consortium. 2017. Phase 2 of catalise: a multinational and multidisciplinary delphi consensus study of problems with language development: Terminology. *Journal of Child Psychology and Psychiatry*, 58(10):1068–1080.

D.V.M. Bishop, Margaret Snowling, Paul Thompson, Trisha Greenhalgh, C. Adams, Lisa Archibald, G. Baird, A. Bauer, J. Bellair, Christopher Boyle, Elizabeth Brownlie, Glenn Carter, B. Clark, Judy Clegg, Nancy Cohen, Gualtiero Nunzi Conti, Julie Dockrell, J. Dunn, Susan Ebbels, and Andrew Whitehouse. 2016. Catalise: A multinational and multidisciplinary delphi consensus study. identifying language impairments in children. *PLoS ONE*, 11.

Joan Bresnan, Anna Cueni, Tatiana Nikitina, and Harald Baayen. 2007. *Predicting the dative alternation*. Royal Netherlands Academy of Science.

Gina Conti-Ramsden and Nicola Botting. 1999. Classification of children with specific language impairment. *Journal of Speech, Language, and Hearing Research*, 42(5):1195–1204.

Walter Daelemans. 2013. Explanation in computational stylometry. In *Proc. of CICLing'13*.

Luna De Bruyne, Ben Verhoeven, and Walter Daelemans. 2018. Stylometric text analysis for dutch-speaking adolescents with autism spectrum disorder. *Computational Linguistics in the Netherlands*, 8:3–23.

Gary S. Dell and Franklin Chang. 2014. The p-chain: Relating sentence production and its disorders to comprehension and acquisition. *Philosophical Transactions of the Royal Society B: Biological Sciences*, 369(1634).

Julie Dockrell, Geoff Lindsay, Olympia Palikara, and Mairi Cullen. 2007. Raising the achievements of children and young people with specific speech and language difficulties and other special educational needs through school to work and college.

Lloyd M. Dunn and Leota M. Dunn. 1997. *The British Picture Vocabulary Scale Second Edition (BPVS II)*. Windsor Berkshire: NFER-NELSON Publication Company.

Colin Elliot, Pauline Smith, and Kay McCullouch. 1996. *The British Ability Scales II (BASII)*. Windsor Berkshire: NFER-NELSON Publication Company.

Charles J. Fillmore. 1976. Frame semantics and the nature of language. *Annals of the New York Academy of Sciences*, 280(1):20–32.

Anouschka Foltz, Kristina Thiele, Dunja Kashnitz, and Prisca Stenneken. 2015. Children's syntactic-priming magnitude: lexical factors and participant characteristics. *Journal of Child Language*, 42(4):932–945.

Courtenay Frazier Norbury, Tracey Gemmell, and Rhea Paul. 2013. Pragmatics abilities in narrative production: A cross-disorder comparison. *Journal of child language*, 41:1–26.

Uta. Frith. 1989. *Autism : explaining the enigma*. Basil Blackwell, Oxford, UK; Cambridge, MA, USA.

Keyur Gabani, Melissa Sherman, Thamar Solorio, Yang Liu, Lisa Bedore, and Elizabeth Peña. 2009. A corpus-based approach for the prediction of language impairment in monolingual english and spanish-english bilingual children. In *Proc. of NAACL-HLT 2009*.

Keyur Gabani, Thamar Solorio, Yang Liu, Khairunnisa Hassanali, and Christine A. Dollaghan. 2011. Exploring a corpus-based approach for detecting language impairment in monolingual english-speaking children. *Artif. Intell. Med.*, 53(3).

Michael S. Gaffrey, Natalia M. Kleinhans, Frank Haist, Natacha Akshoomoff, Ashley Campbell, Eric Courchesne, and Ralph-Axel Müller. 2007. A typical participation of visual cortex during word processing in autism: An fmri study of semantic decision. *Neuropsychologia*, 45(8):1672 – 1684.

Maria Garraffa, Moreno I. Coco, and Holly P. Branigan. 2015. Effects of immediate and cumulative syntactic experience in language impairment: Evidence from priming of subject relatives in children with sli. *Language Learning and Development*, 11(1):18–40.

Maria Garraffa, Moreno I Coco, and Holly P Branigan. 2018. Impaired implicit learning of syntactic structure in children with developmental language disorder: Evidence from syntactic priming. *Autism & Developmental Language Impairments*, 3:2396941518779939.

Erving Goffman. 1979. Frame analysis: An essay on the organization of experience. *Philosophy and Phenomenological Research*, 39(4):601–602.

Micah Goldwater, Marc Tomlinson, Catharine Echols, and Bradley Love. 2011. Structural priming as structure-mapping: Children use analogies from previous utterances to guide sentence production. *Cognitive science*, 35:156–70.

Shelley Gray, Elena Plante, Rebecca Vance, and Mary Henrichsen. 1999. The diagnostic accuracy of four vocabulary tests administered to preschool-age children. *Language, Speech, and Hearing Services in Schools*, 30(2):196–206.

Suzanne Hala, Penny Pexman, and Melanie Glenwright. 2007. Priming the meaning of homographs in typically developing children and children with autism. *Journal of autism and developmental disorders*, 37:329–40.

Francesca Happe and Uta Frith. 2006. The weak coherence account: Detail-focused cognitive style in autism spectrum disorders. *Journal of autism and developmental disorders*, 36:5–25.

L M Henderson, P J Clarke, and M J Snowling. 2011. Accessing and selecting word meaning in autism spectrum disorder. *Journal of Child Psychology and Psychiatry*, 52(9):964–973.

Yoko Kamio, Diana Robins, Elizabeth Kelley, Brook Swainson, and Deborah Fein. 2007. Atypical lexical/semantic processing in high-functioning autism spectrum disorders without early language delay. *Journal of Autism and Developmental Disorders*, 37(6):1116–1122.

EVAN KIDD. 2012. Individual differences in syntactic priming in language acquisition. *Applied Psycholinguistics*, 33(2):393–418.

Diane King, Julie Dockrell, and Morag Stuart. 2014. Constructing fictional stories: a study of story narratives by children with autistic spectrum disorder. *Research in developmental disabilities*, 35(10).

Diane King, Julie E Dockrell, and Morag Stuart. 2013. Event narratives in 11-14 year olds with autistic spectrum disorder. *International Journal of Language & Communication Disorders*, 48(5).

Diane King and Olympia Palikara. 2018a. Assessing language skills in adolescents with autism spectrum disorder. *Child Language Teaching and Therapy*, 34(2):101–113.

Diane King and Olympia Palikara. 2018b. Dataset with narratives by children with developmental language disorder. In Preparation.

Maryellen MacDonald. 2013. How language production shapes language form and comprehension. *Frontiers in Psychology*, 4:226.

Christopher D. Manning, Mihai Surdeanu, John Bauer, Jenny Finkel, Steven J. Bethard, and David Mc-Closky. 2014. The Stanford CoreNLP natural language processing toolkit. In *Proc. of ACL 2014: System Demonstrations*.

Maria Manolitsi and Nicola Botting. 2011. Language abilities in children with autism and language impairment: using narrative as a additional source of clinical information. *Child Language Teaching and Therapy*, 27(1):39–55.

Carol A. Miller and Patricia Deevy. 2006. Structural priming in children with and without specific language impairment. *Clinical Linguistics & Phonetics*, 20(5):387–399. PMID: 16728335.

Laurent Mottron, Karine Morasse, and Sylvie Belleville. 2001. A study of memory functioning in individuals with autism. *Journal of child psychology and psychiatry, and allied disciplines*, 42:253–60.

Courtenay Frazier Norbury and Dorothy V. M. Bishop. 2003. Narrative skills of children with communication impairments. *International Journal of Language & Communication Disorders*, 38(3):287–313.

Emily T Prud'hommeaux, Brian Roark, Lois M Black, and Jan van Santen. 2011. Classification of atypical language in autism. *ACL HLT 2011*.

Pia Rämä, Louah Sirri, and Josette Serres. 2013. Development of lexical–semantic language system: N400 priming effect for spoken words in 18- and 24-month old children. *Brain and Language*, 125(1):1–10.

Michaela Regneri and Diane King. 2015. Automatically evaluating atypical language in narratives by children with autistic spectrum disorder. In *Proc. of NLPCS 2014*.

Michaela Regneri and Diane King. 2016. Automated discourse analysis of narrations by adolescents with autistic spectrum disorder. In *Proceedings of the 7th Workshop on Cognitive Aspects of Computational Language Learning*, pages 1–9. Association for Computational Linguistics.

Michaela Regneri, Alexander Koller, and Manfred Pinkal. 2010. Learning script knowledge with web experiments. In *Proceedings of ACL 2010*, Uppsala, Sweden. Association for Computational Linguistics.

Stefano Rezzonico, Xi Chen, Patricia L. Cleave, Janice Greenberg, Kathleen Hipfner-Boucher, Carla J. Johnson, Trelani Milburn, Janette Pelletier, Elaine Weitzman, and Luigi Girolametto. 2015. Oral narratives in monolingual and bilingual preschoolers with sli. *International Journal of Language & Communication Disorders*, 50(6):830–841.

Mabel L. Rice and Lesa Hoffman. 2015. Predicting vocabulary growth in children with and without specific language impairment: A longitudinal study from 2;6 to 21 years of age. *Journal of Speech Language and Hearing Research*, 58(2):345–359.

Mabel L Rice, Filip Smolik, Denise Perpich, Travis Thompson, Nathan Rytting, and Megan Blossom. 2010. Mean length of utterance levels in 6-month intervals for children 3 to 9 years with and without language impairments. *Journal of Speech, Language, and Hearing Research*.

Masoud Rouhizadeh, Emily Prud'hommeaux, Brian Roark, and Jan van Santen. 2013. Distributional semantic models for the evaluation of disordered language. In *Proc. of NAACL-HLT 2013*.

Masoud Rouhizadeh, Emily Prud'Hommeaux, Jan Van Santen, and Richard Sproat. 2015. Measuring idiosyncratic interests in children with autism. In *Proc. of ACL 2015*.

Roger C. Schank and Robert P. Abelson. 1977. *Scripts, Plans, Goals and Understanding*. Lawrence Erlbaum, Hillsdale, NJ.

Eleanor Semel, Elisabeth .H Wiig, and Wayne Secord. 2006. *Clinical Evaluation of Language Fundamentals (CELF-4 UK)*, fourth edition uk edition. Pearson Assessment.

Nancy L Stein and Elizabeth R Albro. 1997. Building complexity and coherence: Children's use of of goal-structured knowledge in telling stories. *Narrative development: Six approaches*, page 5.

Bruce Tomblin. 2011. Co-morbidity of autism and sli: kinds, kin and complexity. *International Journal of Language & Communication Disorders*, 46(2):127–137.

D. Wetherell, N. Botting, and G. Conti-Ramsden. 2007. Narrative in adolescent specific language impairment (sli): a comparison with peers across two different narrative genres. *International Journal of Language & Communication Disorders*, 42(5):583–605.

Victoria Yaneva, Irina Temnikova, and Ruslan Mitkov. 2015. Accessible texts for autism: An eye-tracking study. In *Proceedings of the 17th International ACM SIGACCESS Conference on Computers & Accessibility*, ASSETS '15, pages 49–57, New York, NY, USA. Association for Computing Machinery.

A Appendix: Story Corpus Excerpt

We are providing the complete story corpus as supplementary material, together with the images and the crowd-sourced language data. In this section, to give an impression of the data, we give examples from this corpus alongside the pictures and prompts presented as stimuli. These include some of the transcribed fictional narratives (King et al., 2014) and some exemplary event narratives (King et al., 2013) from each of the participating groups. The transcriptions preserve all (partially ungrammatical) artifacts of the original spontaneous speech. In some cases, the stories were interrupted by intermediary examiner prompts, which we omit for brevity. Slashes ("/") indicate utterance boundaries. We present the instructions used to collect the original data, and include the images we evaluated as priming sources, which were shown to the subjects in the respective experimental setup. From the story corpus, we present two examples from the ASD and two from the DLD group for each story stem, and one example per control group. Additionally, we show the crowdsourced textual priming cues (for a complete version, see the supplementary data of this paper).

A.1 Corpus Examples: Fictional Narratives

A.1.1 Instructions for participants

The following shows the instructions given to the participants by King et al. (2014) to collect the story corpus:

> I am going to start a story. I'd like you to continue and finish the story. You can use the picture to help you if you like. First, we're going to try a practice one:

> The boy was swimming in the river. On a rock, he saw a strange creature, half man, half fish.

For the corpus collection, the participants were then presented with the story stems shown in the following.

A.1.2 The *Forest* story

The boy ran into the forest. He looked ahead of him and saw a little green man in a spaceship.

ASD

Example 1: the spaceship was quite small. / And the alien was about the size of a small cat. / And it was friendly. / but it didn't really understand how

Figure 1: Picture for the *Forest* story

humans said hello. / So it thought, to say 'hello' you had to vaporise the person in front of you. / and then the boy ran away, shut his door and then decided not to drink anymore whisky or beer.

ASD Example 2: The green man had three eyes. / It had claws and fangs. / It looked at him and ran into the spaceship. / Out came three more green men carrying laser guns, dun dun dun.

DLD

Example 1: The boy. / he just died from a alien . / Okay maybe he banged his head. / and the alien talk XX. / maybe he was unconscious . / I think the alien was experimenting him . / He was out of space for years and years and years . / and he came back like this. / The end. / Just like that. / He turned to them. / he turned to aliens . / To a evil one . / He have a big big brain. / Having one of those things and pale really long, and some legs . / tall, sharp teeth like, and red eyes, as very scary as anything . / and then people saw that. / and they made it as a story . / that they say that in the forest you'll see they named that animal named by the anaconda . / I mean the an part an part the an perd . / The an pert . / Yeah but they say that that is a story. / but it was real . / but I think aliens they were . / he was trying to call them. / but he couldn't . / he did this for years . / He was standing in the forest for years and years and years and years and years . / but he's never gaingame, never been older, ever . / Yeah. / And if anybody goes there and see them, they can't go back. / Yeah, if they go in they can't go out. / So that's the end. / The end.

DLD Example 2: Okay. He runs over to

the spaceship. / And the green man looks behind him and the person gets freaked out . / Trys to run away. / But then the green man captures him in his spaceship and flies off . / And then they do tests on him. / And with stuff. / And then they put him back into the forest. / And then he runs somewhere else. / And then, his mum sees him. / And quickly grabs him and brings him home. / Ya.

Language-Matched Controls:

He was shocked at first because he didn't know what it is. / So he walked up. / and he got suck/ed in by a tractor beam. / and he found himself in a UFO. / he was surround/ed by weird looking creatures like aliens. / and they started speaking like this unknown language to him. / and he couldn't understand a thing about them. / So he tried to escape. / he ran away. / but he couldn't cos—because wherever he went he was surround/ed by aliens. / and they eventually capture/ed him and took him off to Mars. /

Age-Matched Controls:

The little green man waved at him and yelled at him to come and help him with his spaceship which had crashed into the forest after he had lost all his fuel. / The little boy went up to him and said that he didn't know what much he could do because he's obviously not very talented at fixing alien space craft. / so he ran out of the forest went to go get the nearest person he could see. / He then brought him back to the spaceship where the little green man was waiting. / and the man he'd brought back was absolutely amazed. / he went up to the little alien and started speaking with him. / And then after a while he persuaded it to come out of it's spaceship. / and it went to meet the locals who were very very amazed. / and then all the people joined together. / and they pulled his spaceship out of the mud. / and he flew back in it to mars.

A.1.3 The *Mountain* story

When the girl climbed up the mountain, she saw, hidden among the trees, a little wooden house covered in snow.

ASD

Example 1: She went up to the mountain to see the house. / She went inside and had a cup of tea. / After that she can't get out because the snow block/ed the door. / And the men came came in and broke it. / but snow came again. / and then she was stuck. / That's it.

Figure 2: Picture for the *Mountain* story

ASD Example 2: the snow house was was a zombie. / and the zombie / he went up to the door. / and the zombie scared him. / and the zombie went to chase the girl. / and the girl ran away to to her grandma that was climbing up the mountain. / and she screamed and jumped off the mountain

DLD

Example 1: The house looked really beautiful to live in. / They were looking everywhere. / They saw no one in. / so they thought they could live in it . / That's it. / (That's) I said that's it. / Nothing else. / I just want to hurry.

DLD Example 2: Yep. / And she thought I'm gonna go and check it out . / And went up to the house. / And walk inside. / Then she saw no lights. / It was really really dark. / The end. / And then she couldn't find the light. / and she was getting really scared . / And, yeah, the end.

Language-Matched Controls:

She saw it was abandoned. / so she went down to see what it was like. / She peeked inside the window. / and inside there was a pixie . / and then the pixie saw the girl and said 'go away from my window'. / and then he threw a bowl of soup over her. / the little girl went home and said: 'daddy there was a pixie who threw some soup over me'. / and then the dad said 'don't be silly'. / stop telling your little stories'.

Age-Matched Controls:

She walked towards the house. / the house lit up. / lights switched on. / She knocked on the door. / she was cold. / she asked if she could come in. / There was a strange lady come to the door, pimples and spots all over her, mouldy ugly hair and very very small. / she went in. / the lady was actually a witch in disguise. / She grabbed the girl and threw her into the oven. / her friend had also came into the house five minutes later and seen her in the oven. / She had pushed the witch over, got her out and ran off. / they reported it all to the police. / The police came up the next day. / The house was not there.

A.2 Corpus Examples: Event Narratives

For each scenario, we present a general and a specific example from both the ASD and the DLD group, and selected examples (either general or specific) from the control groups.

A.2.1 Instructions for participants

The following shows the instructions given to the participants by King et al. (2013) to collect the event narrative corpus. Both the general and the specific condition were first practiced with one scenario:

> I'm going to ask you to talk about things that people usually do. I'm also going to show you some pictures which you can use to help you if you like. First we'll have a practice question: What usually happens when someone goes shopping?

The prompt for each scenario was a question referring to the scenario. For the general case, the prompt was either about "people" (like in the example) or about "(n) year olds", with n being the age of the child.

The specific narratives were prompted with a question referring to a specific experience of the subject, again with a practice question:

> I'm going to ask you to talk a bit about yourself and things that have happened to you. I'm also going to show you some pictures which you can use to help you if you like. First we'll have a practice question: Can you tell me about a time when you went shopping?

All other prompts then were worded as "Can you tell me about one time when you..." followed by the respective scenario.

A.2.2 Spending free time

(The Story prompt for the specific question in this scenario did not ask for a specific event, but rather for an aggregated answer: "What do you usually to in your free time?")

Figure 3: Picture for the *free time* scenario

ASD

General Example: They paint any pictures they want, that they like. / (Like say) if you wanna try and make a very good artist (like say) a big picture (of er) with (er like) angels singing or something like that / So you try and make it beautiful

ASD Specific Example: I go biking / I go to football / Sometimes I go swimming in the seaside and (uh) in the pool / After that I watch TV and play on my gameboy / And sometimes I (paint) paint / Yeh

DLD

General Example: Play games / Watch TV / (Um, they) they go out / (They go foot) they do football

DLD Specific Example: In my free time. / I normally spend time with my friends playing games. / Sometimes I go to their house. / And that's all. / Yeah.

Control – language-matched, general:

(Twelve year old um) Play computer games or play sports or do any other activities that they like doing / maybe drama class / I don't know / Ballet, things like that.

A.2.3 Being scared

Figure 4: Picture for the *scared* scenario

ASD

General Example: They start to sweat / (So I) I know there's the release of a chemical inside the body / And I know that / (um) I can't really think of anything else.

ASD Specific Example: When I was watching this movie called 'Alien" when I was about five / (Not) not a very good movie to watch when you're five / Maybe now but not then / It was really scary

DLD

General Example: They're like, haahh oh my god / They are screaming / Running / That, all of that / Yeah, that's also, next one please

DLD Specific Example: Scary life / Zombie / Hmm / Hmm /

Control – language-matched, specific:

(Uh) this morning, when I went into the bathroom, there was a big hornet on the ceiling / so I got my mum to kill it / (Uh) not really

A.2.4 Having a birthday

Figure 5: Picture for the *birthday* scenario

ASD

General Example: They blow out candles / Well, that's all I did but I don't know what other people would do on their birthday

ASD Specific Example: (My last one) on my last birthday I went up to York national railway museum / I saw trains / I saw trains (in) in the museum / Just for the birthday weekend really /

DLD

General Example: (Go to like), to go to a holiday / Legoland / I went to Legoland! Go to the funfair / go to see Lego / just build lego / every lego like you do, even here / You went, and even see the other water / Get all your presents / Yeah /

DLD Specific Example: Blowing candle.

Control – age-matched, general:

They have a huge party / bring friends / have cake / (have) get birthday presents from their family / if they have enough money, save up and buy something they really want like a bike, xbox, games, (um) or just spend it on something nice (they really) they've always wanted, I thought / They could sleep out

A.2.5 Going on holdiay

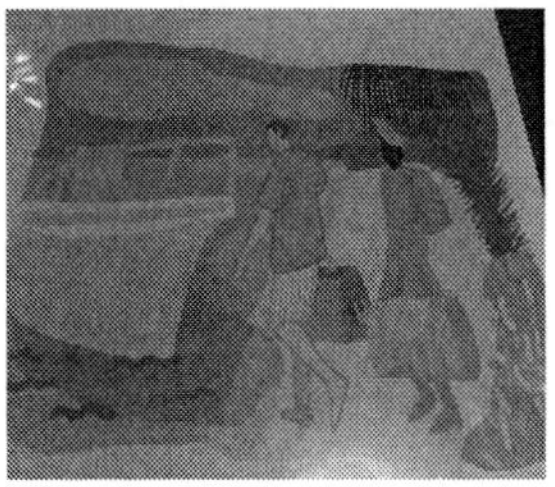

Figure 6: Picture for the *holiday* scenario

ASD

General Example: A different country, pack stuff, and take clothes.

ASD Specific Example: A different country, pack stuff, and take clothes / yeh yeh yeh / I love holidays / get a day of school / school / I like schools / I (like like to) liked last years / liked last years holiday / no / no / lets stop

DLD

General Example: Sometimes they get boat / Or they have their drink or something in the boat and have fun there / See dolphins if in that country / some countries have dolphins, some don't

DLD Specific Example: On the boat / Sand, ocean / Beach / suitcase / bag / hat / swimming shorts and bikini

Control – age-matched, specific

(Uh) when I went on holiday I went to Portugal to my auntie because she was having her wedding anniversary / and we had a big party / and I went for four weeks / (Um) I went swimming in the sea / and (I got) I came out blue

A.2.6 Halloween

ASD

General Example: Carve pumpkins / Don't know / (uh).

ASD Specific Example: Handed out candy to people who came knocking at my door / That's it

Figure 7: Picture for the *halloween* scenario

DLD

General Example: They dress up / And they go trick or treating / And someone knocks on your door you got to give them sweets / dunno
DLD Specific Example: On Halloween I (put up) helped my mum put up pumpkin / And then I went trick or treating

Control – language-matched, general:

Usually, familys who aren't going out will always buy (like) sweets / and usually to show that they're takeing part they have a pumpkin with a candle inside / And people dress and go to other peoples' houses with bags to collect sweets

A.2.7 Being Angry

Figure 8: Picture for the *angry* scenario

ASD

General Example: They either stop being friends with them or something / or they get into a fight / Start japing at each other
ASD Specific Example: I was angry / Beat up someone / And beat up someone else / Be nasty

DLD

General Example: Mmm, hating each other.
DLD Specific Example: Somebody annoying / Somebody annoying

Control – age-matched, specific:

(Um) once I got angry with my friend (um) because (um well) he was geting angry with me / so I got angry with him really / (Uh) I think it was because (um) he wasn't being that nice to anyone that day

so he got angry with me (so) for some reason / I can't really remember

B Supplementary Data

We provide the priming stimuli we evaluated in this study (images and data collected on mechanical turk). The data is accessible under the following url: `https://imagesandimagination.s3.eu-central-1.amazonaws.com/ImagesAndImagination_Supplements.zip` The supplementary material contains a table (`priming_amt_data.tsv`) as tab-separated values with the following columns:

- **Scenario id**: An integer (1-8)

- **type**: *event* (1-6) or *fictional* (7 & 8)

- **name**: A textual description of the scenario

- **script entities**: Entities collected via AMT as prototypically occurring in the given scenario, comma-separated (no spaces)

- **image entities**: Entities collected via AMT that describe the given image

- **image file**: name of the image file for the given scenario

The textual priming cues collected for the two experiments are additionally shown in table 7.

Scenario name	Script-based Cues	Image-based Cues
spending free time	play, video game, friend, football, television, swim, run, park, dance, bike	swim, water, paint, brush, tree, player, game, football, cycle, ball, tv, soccer, play, paint, men, glass, entertainment, computer, bike, art, cloud
being scared	cry, hide, gun, threat, scary, quietness, movie, mother, heavy breath, child, bully, burglar	surprise, man, fear, face, sweater, surprised, shirt, serious, painting, orange, hair, framework, feeling, color, open, blonde
having a birthday	cake, balloons, party ball, music, gift, candle, dance, friend, present, game, family	cake, birthday, plate, candle, celebration, cream, chart, flame, flavour
going on holiday	family, friend, food, drink, beach, suitcase, music, hotel	boat, woman, tree, ship, man, sea, water, vacation, suitcase, sand, beach, trip, sky, luggage, bag, walk, palm, cloud
halloween	candy, costume, treat, pumpkin, skeleton, party, trick	pumpkin, witch, moon, hat, halloween, scary, night, jack-o-lantern, horror, fear, plant
being angry	fight, frowning, crying, yelling, upset, tension, shouting	arguing, boy, smile, pointing, playing, girl, fight, child, anger, argument
forest story	snow, tree, rocks, people, house, fear, dog	forest, alien, ufo, tree, extra terrestrial, spaceship
mountain story	tree, animals, alien, abduction	snow, wood, tree, cabin, forest, windows, quiet, mountain, hut, house, home, cold

Table 7: Priming cues for the different story scenarios crowdsourced via mechanical turk and filtered (cf. Sec. 3)

Production-based Cognitive Models as a Test Suite for Reinforcement Learning Algorithms

Adrian Brasoveanu
UC Santa Cruz, Linguistics
1156 High St., Santa Cruz, CA 95064
abrsvn@gmail.com

Jakub Dotlačil
Utrecht University
Utrecht, The Netherlands
j.dotlacil@gmail.com

Abstract

We introduce a framework in which production-rule based computational cognitive modeling and Reinforcement Learning can systematically interact and inform each other. We focus on linguistic applications because the sophisticated rule-based cognitive models needed to capture linguistic behavioral data promise to provide a stringent test suite for RL algorithms, connecting RL algorithms to both accuracy and reaction-time experimental data. Thus, we open a path towards assembling an experimentally rigorous and cognitively realistic benchmark for RL algorithms. We extend our previous work on lexical decision tasks and tabular RL algorithms (Brasoveanu and Dotlačil, 2020b) with a discussion of neural-network based approaches, and a discussion of how parsing can be formalized as an RL problem.

1 Reinforcement Learning and Production-based Cognitive Models

We introduce a framework in which we can start exploring how Reinforcement Learning (RL; Sutton and Barto 2018) algorithms scale up against human cognitive performance, as captured by complex, production-based cognitive models. Our ultimate goal is to focus on sophisticated cognitive models of linguistic skills, e.g., the parsers in Lewis and Vasishth (2005); Hale (2011); Engelmann (2016), because cognitive models that use theoretically-grounded linguistic representations and processes call for richly structured representations and complex rule systems that pose significant challenges for RL algorithms.

These cognitive models, which capture human-participant accuracy and latency data obtained from forced-choice and reaction-time experiments, can provide exacting, experimentally established benchmarks for the performance of artificial RL agents. These benchmarks will enable us to see if and when different RL algorithms fail, and how exactly they fail. In this paper, we report a small pilot study that exemplifies three modes of failure. Neural-network based function-approximation approaches sometimes (i) fail to learn even fairly simple rule systems in a stable manner. Even when they seem to learn, (ii) they fail by learning a lot of noise (incorrect rules), particularly in more complex tasks. Tabular approaches fare better, but (iii) learn complex tasks much more slowly, and still learn a lot of noise in more complex tasks, albeit less so than neural-network approaches.

Bridging the RL–cognitive modeling divide also promises to shed new light on the issue of cognitive model learnability. The learnability problem for production-rule based models can be divided into two parts: (i) rule acquisition – forming complex rules out of simpler ones, and (ii) rule ordering – deciding which rule to fire when. We focus here on the easier problem of rule ordering, and show how, on one hand, linguistic cognitive models provide a benchmark for RL algorithms and, on the other hand, RL provides a framework to systematically investigate cognitive model learnability in a formally and computationally explicit way.

We investigate the issue of rule-ordering learning using the Adaptive Control of Thought-Rational (ACT-R) cognitive architecture (see Anderson and Lebiere 1998; Anderson 2007). The advantage of using ACT-R is that this cognitive architecture and RL have very close, albeit largely unexplored, connections (Fu and Anderson 2006, Sutton and Barto 2018, Ch. 14). ACT-R tries to address the rule acquisition and ordering problems, but its proposed solutions – production compilation and rule-utility estimation, respectively – have not been systematically applied to complex models for linguistic skills (apart from Taatgen and Anderson 2002, which investigates the role of production compilation in

Proceedings of the Workshop on Cognitive Modeling and Computational Linguistics, pages 28–37
Online Event, November 19, 2020. ©2020 Association for Computational Linguistics
https://doi.org/10.18653/v1/P17

morphology acquisition).

After a brief overview of ACT-R and the description of a linguistic task for which rule-ordering learning will be studied (Section 2), we show how the linguistic task can be analyzed as an RL problem (Section 3), and discuss the results of our experiments with tabular and neural-network based Q-learning algorithms (Section 4). We then briefly discuss how parsing can be formalized as an RL problem (Section 5), and conclude with a summary and some directions for future work (Section 6).

2 Learning Goal-conditioned Rules in Lexical Decision: A Simple Test Case

There are two types of memory in ACT-R. On one hand, we have declarative memory ('knowing that'), which encodes our knowledge of facts. Facts are represented as chunks / attribute-value matrices, e.g., the lexical chunk for the word *elephant*:

$$
(1) \quad \begin{vmatrix} \text{ISA:} & \text{word} \\ \text{FORM:} & \text{elephant} \\ \text{MEANING:} & [\![\text{elephant}]\!] \\ \text{CATEGORY:} & \text{noun} \\ \text{NUMBER:} & \text{sg} \end{vmatrix}
$$

On the other hand, we have procedural memory ('knowing how'), which consists of the set of productions that fire in series to generate cognitive behavior / processes. These productions have the form of rewrite rules in formal grammars (e.g., context free / phrase structure grammars), but in ACT-R, they are conditionalized cognitive actions: the ACT-R mind fires a production, i.e., takes the action encoded in it, if the current cognitive state satisfies the preconditions of that production. Procedural memory and its production rules are the focus of our investigation and RL experiments here.

An example production is provided in (2): if the current cognitive state is such that the goal buffer (which drives cognitive processes in ACT-R) encodes a TASK of 'retrieving' the lexical entry for the FORM 'elephant,' then ($\Longrightarrow$), we take the action of placing a Retrieval (buffer) request to search declarative memory for a word with the FORM 'elephant,' and we consequently update the TASK in the goal buffer to one of 'retrieval done.'

$$
(2) \quad \text{Goal>} \begin{vmatrix} \text{TASK:} & \text{retrieving} \\ \text{FORM:} & \text{elephant} \end{vmatrix} \quad \Longrightarrow
$$

$$
\text{Goal>} \begin{vmatrix} \text{TASK:} & \text{retrieval done} \end{vmatrix}
$$

$$
\text{Retrieval>} \begin{vmatrix} \text{ISA:} & \text{word} \\ \text{FORM:} & \text{elephant} \end{vmatrix}
$$

Implicit in this example production is that an ACT-R mind is composed of modules, which include declarative and procedural memory, but also visual and motor modules etc. Modules are not directly accessible: they can only be accessed through their associated buffers, e.g., the retrieval buffer is associated with declarative memory. Buffers serve a dual purpose: individually, they provide the input/output interface to specific modules; as a whole, however, buffers represent the current cognitive state of the mind. Crucially, productions fire based on the current cognitive state, i.e., they are conditioned on the contents of various buffers.

The ACT-R architecture constrains cognitive behavior in various ways, two of which are that (i) buffers can hold only one chunk, and (ii) only one production can fire at any given time.

The framework and the range of issues that emerge when we try to systematically bridge RL and ACT-R are best showcased with a simple kind of linguistic tasks: lexical decision (LD) tasks. We briefly outline in Section 5 how to extend this approach to parsing models implemented in ACT-R. In an LD task, human participants see a string of letters on a screen. If the participants think the string of letters is a word, they press one key (J in our setup). If they think the string is not a word, they press a different key (F in our setup). After pressing the key, the next stimulus is presented. We will investigate the extent to which two kinds of RL agents can be used to learn goal-conditioned rules in an ACT-R based cognitive model of LD tasks.

The main point of proposing and examining an ACT-R model of LD tasks is to construct a simple example of a production-rule based model that enables us to study learnability issues associated with RL algorithms. Our discussion recapitulates the main results in Brasoveanu and Dotlačil (2020b), and extends them with an initial foray into neural-network based RL approaches. The LD model and RL algorithms can be scaled up in future work to more complex and cognitively realistic syntactic and semantic parsing models, since LD is basically a subcomponent of parsing.

The LD model provides the basic scaffolding of production rules needed for LD tasks, which is all that we need for our purposes: fleshing it out to capture major experimental results about LD, or comparing it to previously proposed cognitive models of LD is not our focus here.

We model three LD tasks of increasing length, hence difficulty: (i) a 1-stimulus task consisting only of the word *elephant*, (ii) a 2-stimuli task consisting of the word *elephant* and a non-word, and (iii) a 4-stimuli task consisting of the word *elephant*, a non-word, the word *dog*, and another non-word.

The model components are split between declarative memory, which stores the lexical knowledge of an English speaker, and procedural memory, which stores rules that enable the model to carry out the LD task. LD tasks can be modeled in ACT-R with a small number of rules (see Brasoveanu and Dotlačil 2019, 2020a). We will assume 4 rules, provided in standard ACT-R format below. These rules were originally hand-coded to fire serially by conditioning all the actions on specific goal states. The goal conditions are stricken out, indicating that goal states were not provided to the RL agents: the order of the rules was not hand-coded for them. Instead, we want the RL agents to learn the rule ordering.

Rule 1: Retrieving

~~goal>~~ | STATE: ~~retrieving~~ |

visual> | VALUE: =val |
| VALUE: ~FINISHED |

$\Longrightarrow$

goal> | STATE: retrieval_done |

+retrieval> | ISA: word |
| FORM: =val |

Rule 2: Lexeme Retrieved

~~goal>~~ | STATE: ~~retrieval_done~~ |

retrieval> | BUFFER: full |
| STATE: free |

$\Longrightarrow$

goal> | STATE: retrieving |

+manual> | CMD: press-key |
| KEY: J |

Rule 3: No Lexeme Found

~~goal>~~ | STATE: ~~retrieval_done~~ |

retrieval> | BUFFER: empty |
| STATE: error |

$\Longrightarrow$

goal> | STATE: retrieving |

+manual> | CMD: press-key |
| KEY: F |

Rule 4: Finished

~~goal>~~ | STATE: ~~retrieving~~ |

visual> | VALUE: FINISHED |

$\Longrightarrow$

goal> | STATE: done |

With fully specified, hand-coded rules, the LD task unfolds as follows. Assume the initial goal STATE of the ACT-R model is `retrieving`, and the word *elephant* appears on the virtual screen of the model, which is automatically stored in the VALUE slot of the visual buffer. At this initial stage, the preconditions of **Rule 1** are satisfied, so the rule fires. This starts an attempt to retrieve a word with the form *elephant* from declarative memory, and the goal STATE is updated to `retrieval_done`. When the word is successfully retrieved, **Rule 2** fires and the J key is pressed. At that point:

i. in the 1-stimulus task, the text FINISHED is displayed, then **Rule 4** fires and ends the task;

ii. in the 2-stimuli task, the non-word is displayed, then **Rule 1** fires again; the retrieval attempt fails since we cannot retrieve a non-word from declarative memory, so **Rule 3** fires and the F key is pressed; at that point, the text FINISHED is displayed, then **Rule 4** fires and ends the task;

iii. in the 4-stimuli task, the first non-word is displayed, **Rule 1** fires again, then, just as in the 2-stimuli task, **Rule 3** fires and the F key is pressed, after which the word *dog* is displayed, **Rule 1** fires for the third time followed by **Rule 2**, which means that the J key is pressed and the second non-word is displayed; then, **Rule 1** fires for the final time, followed by **Rule 3**, which triggers an F-key press, after which the text FINISHED is displayed, so **Rule 4** fires and ends the task.

Thus, the rule sequences for the 3 LD tasks are as shown in (3), assuming fully specified, hand-coded rules. However, as we mentioned, we do not hand-code the goal-state preconditions, indicated by striking out the goal states in the 4 rules above. We only specify the actions (and preconditions associated with buffers other than the goal buffer) and let the RL agents, *which can select any rule at any given time*, learn to carry out the LD tasks.

(3) 1-stim rules: $[1-2]-4$
2-stim rules: $[1-2]-[1-3]-4$
4-stim rules: $[1-2]-[1-3]-[1-2]-[1-3]-4$

We see that *proper rule ordering / sequencing is crucial to successfully completing an LD task*, which is like searching for a path through a maze:

(i) the position in the maze is the current cognitive state of the ACT-R mind, (ii) the possible moves (up, left etc.) are the production rules we can fire, and (iii) a path through the maze is given by the proper sequence of production rules we need to fire to complete the LD task.

3 Rule Ordering as an RL Problem

Markov Decision Processes (MDPs) are the stochastic models of sequential decision-making that form the basis of RL approaches to learning. In an MDP, an agent interacts with its environment and needs to make decisions at discrete time steps $t = 1, 2, \ldots, n$. Defining what counts as the agent and what counts as its environment is part of the modeling process. At every step t, all the information from the past relevant for the current action selection is captured in the current state of the process s_t. This is the Markov property: the future is independent of the past given the current state.

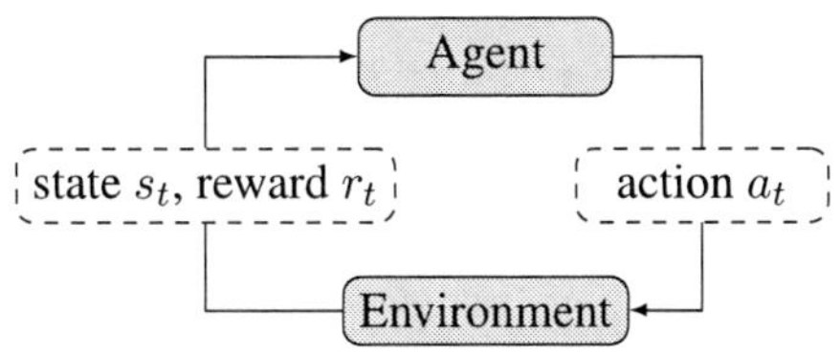

Figure 1: Agent-environment interaction in an MDP

As Figure 1 shows, the environment passes to the agent a state s_t and, at the same time, a reward signal r_t. The agent observes the current state s_t and reward r_t and takes an action a_t, which is passed from the agent to the environment. The cycle then continues: at time step $t + 1$, the environment responds to the agent's action with a new state s_{t+1} and a new reward signal r_{t+1}. Based on these, the agent selects a new action a_{t+1} etc. The definitions of 'state' and 'action' depend on the problem, and are part of the modeling process, just like defining what counts as the agent and its environment.

The agent's *policy* is a complete specification of what action to take at any time step. Given the Markovian nature of the MPD, the policy π is effectively a mapping from the state space S to the action space A, $\pi : S \to A$. A deterministic policy is a mapping from any given state s_t to an action $a_t = \pi(s_t)$, while a stochastic policy is a mapping from any given state s_t to a probability distribution over actions $a_t \sim \pi(s_t)$.

The agent's goal is to maximize some form of cumulative reward over an *episode*, which is a com-plete, usually multi-step interaction between the agent and its environment. In our case, an episode would be a full simulation of a 1/2/4-stim LD task.

The agent learns (solves/optimizes the MDP) by updating its policy π to maximize the (per-episode) cumulative reward. The standard cumulative reward for an episodic task is the discounted return G: at time step $t < n$ (n is the final step in the episode), $G_t = r_{t+1} + \gamma r_{t+2} + \gamma^2 r_{t+3} + \cdots + \gamma^{n-t-1} r_n$, i.e., G_t is the sum of the current reward and the discounted future rewards until the final step n of the episode. Future rewards are discounted in finite / episodic tasks because the agent has a preference for more immediate rewards. The present value of future rewards is determined by the discount factor γ ($0 \leq \gamma \leq 1$). We define the (state-)action value function $Q_\pi(s, a)$ to be the expected (discounted) return when starting in state s, performing action a and then following the policy π until the end of the episode.

The agent selects actions with the goal of maximizing its expected discounted return. If we estimate the Q function for a given policy based on the interactions between the agent and its environment, i.e., based on experience, we can improve that policy by 'greedification:' given a state s, we can always select the optimal action in s, i.e., the action with the maximal expected return according to our current Q estimate.

Q-learning algorithms, which are the focus of our investigation here (given their widespread use), come in various flavors. The simplest one is tabular Q-learning (Watkins, 1989; Watkins and Dayan, 1992), which is fairly effective for our LD tasks. We will also investigate approaches that approximate the Q-function with neural networks, specifically Deep Q-networks (DQN, Mnih and al 2015).

In tabular Q-learning, the Q function $S \times A \to \mathbb{R}$ is represented as a look-up table that stores the estimated values of all possible state-action pairs. The Q table is initialized to an arbitrary fixed value (0). The agent then updates the Q table incrementally at each time step t: the value of the pair (s_t, a_t), where s_t is the state relative to which the agent took action a_t, is updated based on the reward signal r_{t+1} and the new state s_{t+1} that the agent receives back from the environment after taking action a_t.

Q-learning is a form of temporal difference (TD) learning, as shown in (4). The Q^{new} value estimate for the state-action pair (s_t, a_t) is based on the Q^{old} value, updated by some proportion α (the learning rate; $0 < \alpha \leq 1$) of the TD error.

$$(4) \quad Q^{new}(s_t, a_t) \leftarrow Q^{old}(s_t, a_t) + \alpha \cdot$$

$$\overbrace{\left(r_{t+1} + \gamma \cdot \underbrace{\max_{a_{t+1}} Q^{old}(s_{t+1}, a_{t+1})}_{\text{next-state value estimate}} - Q^{old}(s_t, a_t) \right)}^{\text{TD (temporal difference) error}}$$

$$\underbrace{\phantom{\left(r_{t+1} + \gamma \cdot \max_{a_{t+1}} Q^{old}(s_{t+1}, a_{t+1}) - Q^{old}(s_t, a_t) \right)}}_{\text{TD target (updated value)}}$$

The TD error is the difference between the TD target – which is an updated estimate of the value of the (s_t, a_t) pair – and the Q^{old} value estimate. The TD target consists of (i) the reward r_{t+1} the agent receives after action a_t, which is part of the new data the agent gets back from the environment after action a_t, plus (ii) the estimate of the value of the next state s_{t+1}, where the next state s_{t+1} is the other part of the new data the agent gets back from the environment after action a_t. The Q-learning optimal estimate for the value of the next state s_{t+1} is discounted by γ, since this state is in the future relative to the state-action pair (s_t, a_t) we're currently updating. This optimal estimate for s_{t+1} is aggressively confident / optimistic (in contrast to Expected Sarsa, for example; see van Seijen et al. 2009): the agent looks at all the possible actions a_{t+1} that can be taken in state s_{t+1} and assumes that the action a_{t+1} with the highest Q^{old}-value provides an accurate estimate of the s_{t+1} value.

For tabular Q-learning, the agent (in the RL sense) is a Q-value table that assigns values to all possible state-action pairs and that guides the rule selection process at every cognitive step. The environment is the cognitive state of the ACT-R model / mind, which could conceivably consist of (i) all the modules (procedural memory, declarative memory and visual and motor modules) together with (ii) their associated buffers (goal, retrieval, visual-what, visual-where and the manual buffer). This, however, would lead to a very large state space S, which in turn would lead to a large Q-value table. DQN and similar neural-network approaches can help with the large state-space problem, but we will nonetheless take a state s to consist just of: (i) the goal buffer, (ii) the retrieval buffer, (iii) the value in the visual-what buffer, if any, and finally, (iv) the state of the manual buffer (busy or free). For example, the state after the word *elephant* is retrieved from declarative memory is: goal: {STATE: retrieval_done}, retrieval: {FORM: elephant}, visual_value: elephant, manual: free.

The action space consists of the 4 rules above,

namely `retrieving`, `lexeme retrieved`, `no lexeme found` and `finished`, together with a special action None that the agent selects when it wants to not fire any rule because it prefers to wait for a new cognitive state.

The reward structure is as follows: (i) the agent receives a positive reward of 1 at the end of an episode (when the LD task is completed), specifically, when the goal STATE is done; (ii) the agent receives a negative reward of -0.15 for every rule it selects, other than None; (iii) there is no penalty for waiting and selecting no rule, i.e., for selecting the special action None, which is optimal when waiting for retrieval requests from declarative memory to complete, for example; (iv) finally, at every step, the agent receives a negative reward equal to the amount of time that has elapsed between the immediately preceding step and the current step (multiplied by -1 to make it negative).

This reward structure is designed to encourage the agent to finish the task as soon as possible by selecting the smallest number of rules. The negative temporal reward (iv) discourages the agent from just repeatedly selecting an action, e.g., None. This ends up timing out the LD task in a small number of steps and fast-forwards the agent to the maximum waiting time per stimulus the ACT-R environment allows for, which we set to 2 seconds per word for the LD task.

Thus, given a simple reward structure that incorporates fairly minimal cognitive assumptions, RL enables us to induce proper rule sequences to complete the LD tasks: RL enables us to *leverage the simple assumptions built into the reward structure to solve the much harder rule-ordering problem by direct experience / trial-and-error interaction* with the LD tasks.

4   Experiments and Results

We assume the usual ACT-R defaults, e.g., rule firing time is set to 50 ms. The discount factor γ is set to 0.95 and the learning rate α is set to 10^{-3}. We use an ϵ-greedy policy to balance exploration and exploitation, with ϵ annealed from a maximum of 1 to a minimum of 0.01.

We investigate two types of agents / algorithms: (i) tabular Q-learning (the main results for tabular agents are from Brasoveanu and Dotlačil 2020b), and (ii) DQN. To a large extent, the agents learn by trial and error to successfully carry out the LD tasks: they learn how to properly order the rules

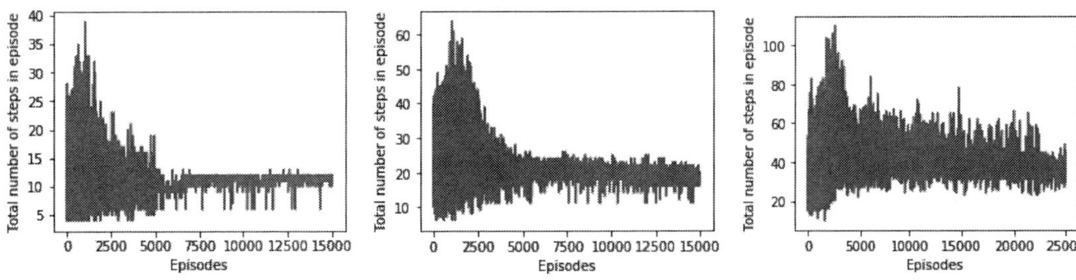

Figure 2: Tabular Q: Steps per episode for the 1-stim (left), 2-stim (middle) and 4-stim (right) tasks

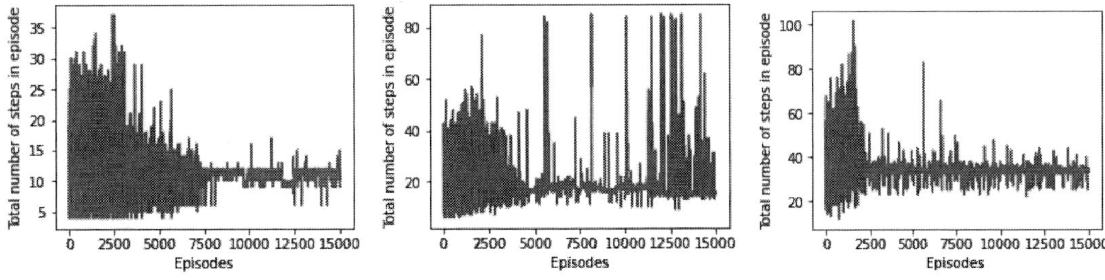

Figure 3: DQN: Steps per episode for 1-stim (left), 2-stim (middle) and 4-stim (right) tasks

and complete the LD tasks as efficiently as possible. This is no small feat given that the actual number of steps, i.e., decision points, when the agents needs to select an action, is larger than the high-level sequences of rule firings in (3) above. For example, for a 1-stim task, there are actually 12 steps where the agent needs to decide whether to wait or to fire a specific rule (when the agent does not complete the task perfectly, it might take much more than 12 steps). The 2-stim task requires 18 such steps (if perfectly completed), and the 4-stim task requires 34 steps (again, if perfectly completed).

The reason for the higher number of steps compared to the number of rules is that our LD simulations involve the visual and motor modules (to read strings of characters and to press keys) in addition to the declarative memory module. Visual and motor actions, just as retrievals from declarative memory, take time, and the agent needs to make decisions while waiting for them to complete.

4.1 Tabular Q-learning in LD Tasks

The higher the number of steps, i.e., the higher number of decision points for the tabular agent, the harder the task is to learn for the tabular agents. As the plots in Figure 2 show, repeated from Brasoveanu and Dotlačil (2020b), learning is faster and less noisy for shorter tasks (fewer stimuli), but the tabular Q-learning agent manages to learn even

the most complex 4-stimuli task moderately well.

We simulate 15,000 episodes, i.e., 15,000 LD decision tasks consisting of 1 stimulus only (the word *elephant*), from which the tabular Q agent learns – shown in the leftmost plot in Figure 2. After about 5,000 episodes, the task is completed in ≈ 12 steps, which is the length of the task when completed perfectly. For some episodes, the number of steps is smaller than 12. In these cases, the agent times out the task (e.g., by selecting the None action several times) and receives steep negative temporal rewards leading to low returns.

A close examination of the agent's final Q-value table, which stores the agent's rule-firing preferences for any given state, indicates that the agent has learned goal-conditioned rules perfectly. We only look at states for which at least one action/rule has a non-0 value (recall that all Q-values are initialized to 0). For each such state, we identify the action/rule with the highest value. There are 8 states total with at least one non-0 value action, and the maximum-value action for each of these states makes complete sense. For example, None is the maximum-value rule at the beginning of every episode when the agent waits for some text to be automatically detected and stored in the visual buffer. Similarly, after a retrieval request is placed, the agent waits for the process to complete.

As the middle plot in Figure 2 shows, we also

simulate 15,000 2-stim episodes (LD tasks consisting of the word *elephant* and the non-word *not_a_word*). After about 9,000 episodes, the task is completed in $\approx$ 18 steps, which is the length of this task when the agent completes it perfectly. A close examination of the agent's final Q-value table indicates that the agent has learned goal-conditioned rules almost perfectly. Once again, we only look at states for which at least one action has a non-0 value – a total of 13 states. For each state, we identify the maximum-value action, and for 12 states, this action makes complete sense. However, unlike in the 1-stim task, there is one state-action pair that encodes a questionable rule. We see here how, for more complex tasks, the tabular RL agents learn spurious rules, which are a by-product of the noisy trial-and-error learning process.

This lack of robust learning, which can be characterized as overgeneralization, or as vulnerability to 'adversarial' inputs, becomes even more prominent in the 4-stim task, where the tabular Q-learning agent learns even more spurious rules. As the rightmost plot in Figure 2 shows, we simulate 25,000 4-stim episodes (LD tasks consisting of the word *elephant*, a non-word, the word *dog* and another non-word). We need more episodes for this task because it is longer, hence more complex, than the 1/2-stim tasks. It takes about 22,000 episodes for the task to be reliably completed in less than 40 steps. The task takes 34 steps when the agent completes it perfectly, but even after 25,000 episodes, the agent takes more steps than that because it tries incorrect rules or waits for no reason. An examination of the final Q-value table indicates that the agent has learned goal-conditioned rules fairly well, but there is also a good amount of spurious rules. There are 24 states total with at least one action with a non-0 value. Out of these, 6 states have questionable / nonsensical maximum-value actions.

4.2 DQN in LD Tasks

The DQN agents use an artificial neural network (ANN) to approximate the Q-function. We use a simple multilayer perceptron with a hidden layer of size 64. A small hyperparameter search indicated that a hidden size of 32 seems to be too small, while 128 or 256, for example, seems to be too large.

The ANNs are trained using 1-step semi-gradient TD (a.k.a. semi-gradient TD(0); Sutton and Barto 2018, Chapters 9-11), with the Adam optimizer (Kingma and Ba, 2015) and a mean squared TD

error loss function (see (4) above for the TD error).

As the leftmost plot in Figure 3 shows, the DQN agent takes longer than the tabular agent to learn the 1-stim task, but it completes it more or less perfectly after about 7,500 episodes. We inspect the Q-function approximation encoded by the ANN at the end of the simulation by identifying the maximum-value rule for each of the 36 possible states. Unlike tabular approaches, function-approximation approaches aggressively generalize over states by design, which is why they are appropriate for large state (and action) spaces. The final Q-function approximation aggressively generalizes by taking the `finished` rule to be the maximum value action for 31 out of 36 states. This makes sense given that the `finished` rule is immediately followed by the final positive reward of 1.

The other rules are triggered largely only when they are appropriate. For example, the `lexeme retrieved` rule is triggered only in one state – immediately after the word 'elephant' is successfully retrieved from declarative memory. The `None` rule is only triggered in two states: when the agent is waiting for the visual module to auto-detect and encode the text on the virtual screen, and when waiting for the retrieval request to declarative memory to complete. But the DQN agent overgeneralizes the `retrieving` rule. It is appropriately triggered after the text on the virtual screen is stored in the visual buffer, i.e., when visual value is the word 'elephant,' but it is also triggered in one other state when the `None` rule is appropriate because the agent is waiting for the visual module to auto-detect the text on the virtual screen.

As the middle plot in Figure 3 shows, the DQN agent fails to learn the 2-stim task in a stable manner. We tried several different random seeds, and the DQN agent exhibits unstable learning in most of them, sometimes to an even larger extent than depicted here. An examination of the final Q-function approximation reveals that, once again, the `finished` rule is the maximum value action for the vast majority of states (37 out of 48). The `None` rule is triggered only in 4 states. In two of them, the agent is waiting for the visual module to auto-detect the text on the virtual screen and encode it in the visual buffer (whether the manual buffer is free or busy). In another one, the agent is waiting for the retrieval request associated with the non-word to complete. However, the DQN agent has not learned that `None` should also be triggered when waiting for the retrieval request associated with 'elephant,' and it incorrectly triggers None in a state where retrieving is more appropriate.

The lexeme retrieved rule is triggered in 3 states. One of them is the expected one: immediately after the word 'elephant' is successfully retrieved from declarative memory. Another one is a reasonable overgeneralization to a state that is exactly the same as the first one except that the visual value is the non-word. In the third state, however, the None rule is more appropriate since the retrieval process for the word 'elephant' is still in progress. The agent has clearly not learned when to trigger the no lexeme found rule, which is triggered in only one state for which the retrieving rule is appropriate (since the word 'elephant' has just been read off the virtual screen). Finally, the retrieving rule is triggered in 3 states, one of which is appropriate as it immediately follows the point at which the non-word has been read off the virtual screen. However, the DQN agent also triggers this rule in two other states, for which it does not make much sense.

As the rightmost plot in Figure 3 shows, the DQN agent seems to performs much better than the tabular Q agent on the 4-stim task, learning to complete it efficiently after about 2,000 episodes. But an examination of the final Q-function approximation reveals an unexpected result: the retrieving rule is aggressively overgeneralized to 82 states (out of 108). The finished rule is the maximum value action for 9 states only, the lexeme retrieved rule for 8 states, the None rule for 7 states, and the no lexeme found rule for 2 states.

The finished rule is mostly triggered in states in which the visual value is FINISHED (5 out of 9 states), but it is also incorrectly triggered in states in which the 4 stimuli are stored in the visual buffer. It is not clear at all that the agent has learned this rule. The lexeme retrieved rule exhibits a similar profile. It is correctly triggered when the retrieval process for the two words are completed successfully, but there is a lot of noise also: 6 out of 8 states are not states in which this rule should be clearly triggered, and in two of them, the retrieval buffer is empty. Thus, it is far from clear that the agent has learned the lexeme retrieved rule.

The None rule is appropriately triggered when the agent is waiting for the visual module to auto-detect text on the virtual screen, and when waiting

for retrieval requests to complete for the two words 'elephant' and 'dog.' However, the agent has not learned to trigger this rule when waiting for retrieval requests associated with the two non-words. In addition, this rule is overgeneralized to several states where the retrieving rule is more appropriate. Finally, the DQN agent has clearly learned the no lexeme found rule: it is triggered in only two states, after failed retrieval requests associated with the two non-words.

In conclusion, we see that the DQN agent fails to learn the 2-stim task in a stable manner, learns the 1-stim task more slowly than the tabular Q agent, but exhibits an interesting behavior on the 4-stim task. This task seems to be learned very quickly (compared to tabular Q), but there is a very significant amount of noise in the final Q-function approximation. It is therefore not clear that the appropriate preconditions for most of the rules have actually been learned.

5 Parsing as an RL Problem

In this section, we briefly discuss how parsing can be formalized as an RL problem. Just as the LD task, the parsing task can be implemented in ACT-R (cf. Lewis and Vasishth 2005; Brasoveanu and Dotlačil 2018, 2020a). The parser components are split over various ACT-R modules and buffers: (i) lexical knowledge is encoded in declarative memory, (ii) knowledge of grammar and parsing actions are encoded in procedural memory, (iii) expectations about upcoming syntactic categories are encoded in the goal buffer, (iv) information about the current partially-built syntactic parse is encoded in the imaginal buffer (a secondary goal-like buffer), and finally, (v) visual information from the environment is transferred via the visual buffer.

We consider a simple example, which features an eager left-corner parser (Resnik, 1992). Assume we have a simple grammar with four phrase structure rules: (i) S → NP VP, (ii) NP → Det N, (iii) VP → V, (iv) VP → V NP. Also, assume that we are reading the sentence *A boy sleeps* word by word. As shown in Figure 4, we start with the empty visual buffer and our goal stack (the stack of the expected syntactic categories) consists of just S: our goal is to parse a sentence.

We then shift focus to the first word, the information is transferred to the goal buffer, at which point we retrieve its syntactic category Det(erminer) from declarative memory. We can now take a series

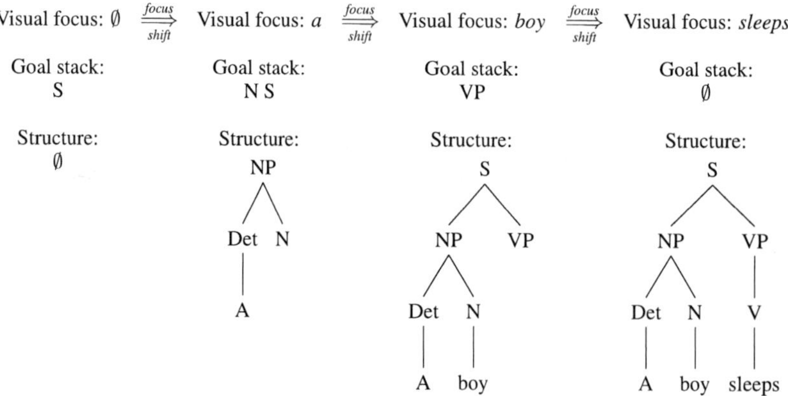

Figure 4: Partial trees built incrementally when reading the sentence *A boy sleeps* word by word

of cognitive steps – that is, we fire a series of productions – that lead to a new state. The new goal stack is N S: we now have the subgoal of finding a N(oun) on the way to S. Also, we build a partial syntactic structure of the form shown in the leftmost tree in Figure 4, and store it in the imaginal buffer. The noun *boy* is then brought into focus, its syntactic category N is retrieved, and we discharge the N goal at the top of the goal stack. At this point, we have the full corner of the rule S $\rightarrow$ NP VP, so we trigger it, which eagerly discharges the S goal and replaces it with the goal of finding a VP (verb phrase). At the same time, a richer partial tree, shown in the middle of Figure 4, is stored in the imaginal buffer. Finally, the verb *sleeps* is in focus, its syntactic category V is retrieved from declarative memory, and we trigger the rule VP $\rightarrow$ V that discharges the VP goal, resulting in an empty goal stack and the rightmost tree structure in Figure 4.

We see that rule ordering plays two roles in parsing. First, the parser has to correctly sequence actions per word: it has to collect the visual information, move it to the goal buffer, recall lexical information from the declarative memory, carry out a parsing action and move its visual attention to the following word. This sequencing of actions is akin to the one explored in the LD task. In addition, the parser has to find the right path through the sequence of parsing rules, e.g., it has to realize that the Det element at the start of the sentence should trigger the NP $\rightarrow$ Det N rule, followed by discharging the N goal etc. Incorrect sequencing would eventually lead to a dead end. For example, had the parser triggered the VP $\rightarrow$ V NP rule when parsing *sleeps*, it would incorrectly end up with an expectation for a non-existent direct object.

6 Summary and Future Work

We argued that sophisticated production-based cognitive models used to capture human behavioral data (particularly linguistic behavior) promise to provide a stringent test suite for RL algorithms. An immediate follow-up would be to explore how RL algorithms perform on a variety of production-based cognitive models, whether linguistic, e.g., syntactic or semantic parsing, or non-linguistic. We have conducted pilot experiments with simple parsing models and tasks, and they are much more difficult than the LD tasks explored in this paper.

Another direction for future research is investigating other value-based tabular learning algorithms (Sarsa, Expected Sarsa), as well as extensively studying ANN-based function-approximation approaches to reinforcement learning, both value and policy based.

Similarly, we might want to investigate curriculum learning (see Elman 1993; Rusu and al 2016 among others) for increasingly complex tasks. A DQN agent that has already learned the 1-stim task might be able to learn the 2/4-stim tasks quickly and well. Curriculum or transfer learning might also enable agents to learn from much fewer interactions, and/or from explicit instructions.

Acknowledgments

We are grateful to three anonymous CMCL 2020 reviewers for their feedback on an earlier version of this paper, the NVIDIA Corporation for a grant of two Titan V GPUs used for this research, and the UCSC OR and THI for a matching grant for additional hardware. The usual disclaimers apply.

References

John R. Anderson. 2007. *How can the human mind occur in the physical universe?* Oxford University Press.

John R. Anderson and Christian Lebiere. 1998. *The Atomic Components of Thought*. Lawrence Erlbaum Associates, Hillsdale, NJ.

Adrian Brasoveanu and Jakub Dotlačil. 2018. An extensible framework for mechanistic processing models: From representational linguistic theories to quantitative model comparison. In *Proceedings of the 2018 International Conference on Cognitive Modelling*.

Adrian Brasoveanu and Jakub Dotlačil. 2019. Quantitative comparison for generative theories. In *Proceedings of the 2018 Berkeley Linguistic Society 44*.

Adrian Brasoveanu and Jakub Dotlačil. 2020a. *Computational Cognitive Modeling and Linguistic Theory*. Language, Cognition, and Mind (LCAM) Series. Springer (Open Access).

Adrian Brasoveanu and Jakub Dotlačil. 2020b. Reinforcement learning for production-based cognitive models. In *Proceedings of the 2020 International Conference on Cognitive Modelling*.

Jeffrey L. Elman. 1993. Learning and development in neural networks: The importance of starting small. *Cognition*, 48:71–99.

Felix Engelmann. 2016. *Toward an integrated model of sentence processing in reading*. Ph.D. thesis, University of Potsdam, Potsdam.

Wai-Tat Fu and John R. Anderson. 2006. From recurrent choice to skill learning: A reinforcement-learning model. *Journal of Experimental Psychology: General*, 135(2):184–206.

John Hale. 2011. What a rational parser would do. *Cognitive Science*, 35:399–443.

Diederik P. Kingma and Jimmy Lei Ba. 2015. Adam: A method for stochastic optimization. In *3rd International Conference on Learning Representations, ICLR 2015, San Diego, CA, USA, May 7-9, 2015, Conference Track Proceedings*.

Richard Lewis and Shravan Vasishth. 2005. An activation-based model of sentence processing as skilled memory retrieval. *Cognitive Science*, 29:1–45.

Volodymyr Mnih and al. 2015. Human-level control through deep reinforcement learning. *Nature*, 518(7540):529–533.

Philip Resnik. 1992. Left-corner parsing and psychological plausibility. In *Proceedings of the Fourteenth International Conference on Computational Linguistics*, Nantes, France.

Andrei A. Rusu and al. 2016. Progressive neural networks.

Richard S Sutton and Andrew G Barto. 2018. *Reinforcement learning: An introduction*. MIT press.

Niels A. Taatgen and John R. Anderson. 2002. Why do children learn to say "broke"? a model of learning the past tense without feedback. *Cognition*, 86(2):123–155.

H. van Seijen, H. van Hasselt, S. Whiteson, and M. Wiering. 2009. A theoretical and empirical analysis of Expected Sarsa. In *IEEE Symposium on Adaptive DP and RL*, pages 177–184.

Christopher J. C. H. Watkins and Peter Dayan. 1992. Q-learning. *Machine Learning*, 8(3):279–292.

Christopher John Cornish Hellaby Watkins. 1989. *Learning from Delayed Rewards*. Ph.D. thesis, King's College, Cambridge, UK.

Evaluating Word Embeddings for Language Acquisition

Raquel G. Alhama[1,2] **Caroline Rowland**[1,3] **Evan Kidd**[1,3,4,5]

[1]Language Development Department, Max Planck Institute for Psycholinguistics
[2]Department of Cognitive Science & Artificial Intelligence, Tilburg University
[3]Donders Institute for Brain, Cognition & Behaviour, Radboud University
[4]The Australian National University
[5]ARC Centre of Excellence for the Dynamics of Language
`rgalhama@tilburguniversity.edu,`
`{caroline.rowland,evan.kidd}@mpi.nl`

Abstract

Continuous vector word representations (or word embeddings) have shown success in capturing semantic relations between words, as evidenced by evaluation against behavioral data of adult performance on semantic tasks (Pereira et al., 2016). Adult semantic knowledge is the endpoint of a language acquisition process; thus, a relevant question is whether these models can also capture *emerging* word representations of young language learners. However, the data for children's semantic knowledge across development is scarce. In this paper, we propose to bridge this gap by using Age of Acquisition norms to evaluate word embeddings learnt from child-directed input. We present two methods that evaluate word embeddings in terms of (a) the semantic neighbourhood density of learnt words, and (b) convergence to adult word associations. We apply our methods to bag-of-words models, and find that (1) children acquire words with fewer semantic neighbours earlier, and (2) young learners only attend to very local context. These findings provide converging evidence for validity of our methods in understanding the prerequisite features for a distributional model of word learning.

1 Introduction

Word embeddings have a long tradition in Computational Linguistics. There exist a range of methods to derive word embeddings based on the distributional paradigm, such that words with similar embeddings are semantically related. These embeddings are often evaluated either extrinsically, on how well they boost performance on a certain task, or intrinsically, by comparing representations against behavioral data from tests of semantic similarity, synonymity, analogy or word association (Pereira et al., 2016).

Adult semantic knowledge is the culmination of a language acquisition process; therefore, a relevant question is whether these models can also capture *emerging* word representations of language learners. A capacity for distributional analysis is a basic assumption of all theories of language acquisition: children are capable of performing distributional analyses over their input from a young age (Saffran et al., 1996), motivating the use of word embeddings for modelling language acquisition. However, the evaluation of emergent word representations is far from straightforward, as there is no availability of the kind of semantic judgements that we have for adults.

This paper presents two methods for evaluating word embeddings for language acquisition. We apply our methods to two bag-of-words models, and evaluate them on the acquisition of nouns in English-speaking children[1].

2 Models

Bag-of-words models offer a good starting point to evaluate word representations in the context of language acquisition, given their minimal assumptions on knowledge of word order: once the context of a word is determined, the order in which words appear in this context is ignored by these type of models. We explore a range of hyperparameter configurations of two models: a 'context-counting' model involving a PPMI matrix compressed with Singular Value Decomposition (SVD), and the Skipgram with Negative Sampling (SGNS)

---

[1]We share the code for these methods at `https://github.com/rgalhama/wordrep_cmcl2020`

Proceedings of the Workshop on Cognitive Modeling and Computational Linguistics, pages 38–42
Online Event, November 19, 2020. ©2020 Association for Computational Linguistics
https://doi.org/10.18653/v1/P17

version of *word2vec* (Mikolov et al., 2013). Note that, although these models have been found to implicitly optimize the same shifted-PPMI matrix (Levy and Goldberg, 2014), they are unlikely to obtain the same results without careful parameter alignment. Our goal by selecting these two approaches is to increase the variability of model performance within the bag-of-words paradigm.

The hyperparameters we explore include: window size [1,2,3,4,5,7,10], minimum frequency threshold [10,50,100], dynamic window (for SGNS), negative sampling in SGNS [0,15] (and its equivalents as shifted-PPMI), eigenvalue in SVD [0,0.5,1]. We restrict our analyses to vectors of size 100. We use the Hyperwords package from Levy et al. (2015).

3 Data

We trained the models on transcriptions of child-directed speech, i.e. samples of naturalistic productions in the linguistic environment of a child. We extracted the child-directed speech data from the CHILDES database (MacWhinney, 2000), for all the varieties of English, for ages ranging from 0 to 60 months. We used the `childesr` library to extract the child-directed utterances (Sanchez et al., 2019) [2]. Word tokens were coded at the lemma level. The resulting dataset contains a total number of 3,135,822 sentences, 34,961 word types, and 12,975,520 word tokens.

To evaluate the models, we used data collected with the MacArthur-Bates Communicative Development Inventory forms (CDI). These are forms, given to parents of young children, that contain checklists of common early acquired words. Parents complete the forms according to whether their child *understands* or *produces* each of those words. These forms are collected at different ages, and thus can be used to estimate the Age of Acquisition (AoA) of words. We used all the variants of English 'Words & Sentences' CDIs from the Wordbank database (Frank et al., 2017), with the exception of those involving twins (as significant differences have been observed in the language development of twins and singletons, Tomasello et al., 1986). We estimated the AoA of a word by considering that a word is acquired at the age at which at least 50% of the children in the sample produced a given word.

<hr>

[2] `http://childes-db.stanford.edu/about.html`

4 Method 1: Neighbourhood Density

Our first evaluation method is inspired by prior work on human word learning, presented in Hills et al. (2010). In their work, the authors modeled the emerging network of semantic associations that children build during language acquisition. Their model consists of a simple word co-occurrence matrix, where all the counts greater than zero are flattened into a count of one, resulting in a binary matrix. The authors view the resulting matrix as a network of associations, where words are connected only if they have co-occurred. The number of connections of each word is then used as an index, which the authors call Contextual Diversity (CD). This index has been repeatedly shown to predict language acquisition phenomena, such as the age of acquisition of words in different syntactic categories (Hills et al., 2010; Stella et al., 2017) and individual differences between typically developing children and late talkers (Beckage et al., 2011).

We propose a variant evaluation method that takes *token* co-occurrences into account. Because of the binarization of the co-occurrence matrix, the CD index is an indicator of *type* co-occurrences, and is therefore agnostic to co-occurrence frequency. The models we work with, on the contrary, are sensitive to co-occurrence frequencies, providing a more fine-grained characterization of the semantic space.

Our method works as follows. First, we derived the semantic networks based on the cosine distance between representations. This required us to set a minimum cosine similarity threshold θ to determine if two words are connected, which we treat as a hyperparameter (with values [.6, .7, .8, .9]). Second, given this network, we counted the number of neighbours of each word as the number of other words connected to it. We refer to this index as neighbourhood density (ND). Third, we computed the Pearson's r correlation between this index and the AoA norms.

Figure 1 shows the distribution of the computed metric. Note that these correlations cannot be expected to be of the same order as those found when evaluating against adult ratings, since age of acquisition is predicted by a variety of factors, of which distributional information is only one, and it is subject to greater individual differences than adult semantic knowledge. Therefore, moderate but significant correlations are generally consid-

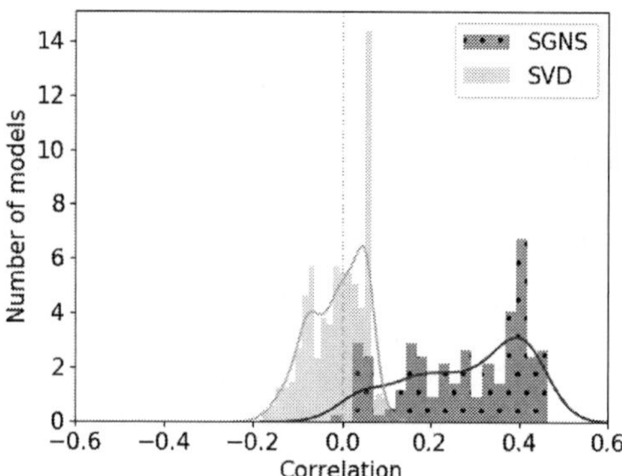

Figure 1: Histogram of Pearson's r correlations between ND and AoA, for SGNS and SVD models.

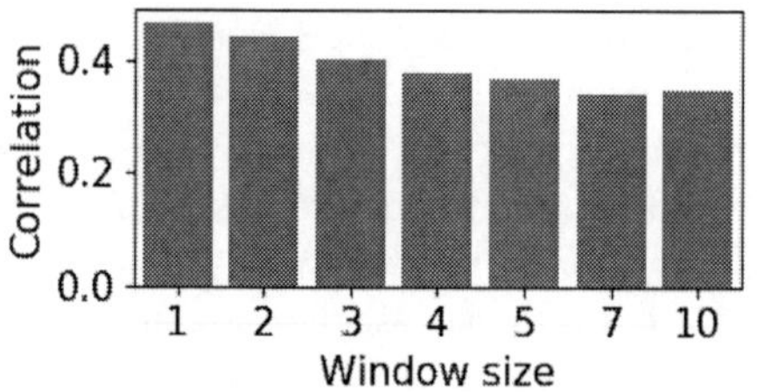

Figure 2: Pearson's r correlation depending on window size, for the best-performing SGNS model.

ered meaningful. As a reference, the CD index, has a correlation of $r = 0.32$ in our dataset [3].

As can be seen, the SGNS model is more likely to provide a semantic space that correlates with AoA, and some configurations yield an effect size comparable (even larger) than the CD metric. This indicates that the SGNS model builds word representations in a way that reflects the relative difficulty of each word, and thus offers a good starting point for understanding how children use distributional context for vocabulary acquisition. The fact that the correlation is positive prompts the prediction that, when co-occurrence frequency is incorporated in the model, words inhabiting less dense neighbourhoods are acquired earlier. This finding suggests that semantic neighbours may act as competitors in the process of word learning.

Among the hyperparameters of these models, one that is particularly relevant to language acquisition is the window size, as this reveals the amount of context that children most likely attend to in the analyzed ages. To investigate this, we took the best model of our previous analyses (SGNS with window size 1, negative sampling 15, frequency threshold 10), and varied only the window size. Results are in figure 2. As can be seen, smaller window sizes have better correlation with the data, indicating that the exploited context at this age is very local. Such a result makes intuitive sense in the context of children's immature verbal memory spans, which only improve as they acquire more language.

---

[3]We replicated the original analyses, since we use an extended dataset (both in the case of CHILDES and the AoA norms).

5   Method 2: Word Associates

Our first evaluation method above focused on the structure of the semantic spaces provided by the learnt word embeddings. Now we turn our attention to the specific lexical items and their position in the semantic space.

Children tend to under- and overextend word meaning in the first stages of acquisition, and over time they become more precise on capturing the semantics of words. A logical assumption then, is that words learnt earlier also converge earlier to adult-like semantic representations (assuming that early and late words take, on average, approximately the same amount of time to converge). We incorporated this idea in our second method by relating the AoA of words with adult free word association norms. Note that this method can be applied to other semantic tasks, but we focus on word association because it does not impose the specific type of semantic relation that words need to have (i.e. there is no distinction between similarity, analogy or others).

The dataset of free word association that we used is known as Small World of Worlds (SWOW, De Deyne et al., 2019), and it is the largest dataset of word associations in English, containing responses to over 12,000 cue words. We filtered the preprocessed version of the dataset to include only words that have been acquired before 60 months old. This results in 613 cue words, and 1839 responses (word associates) to these cues.

We then performed a similar cue-response experiment, with the best model from the previous section: for each cue, we retrieved the closest n neighbours. As in Pereira et al. (2016), we used $n = 50$, and then computed how many of these neighbours overlap with the word associates (responses) provided by human adults. However, unlike that work, our evaluation is not based directly on the number of overlaps. Instead, we computed the Spearman rank correlation between the number of overlaps and the AoA norms, in order to quantify whether word embeddings corresponding to words learned earlier by children are also those that are converging faster to adult semantic knowledge. Figure 3 shows the result of this procedure. As can be seen, there is a statistically significant rank correlation ($\rho = -0.378$, $p < 0.001$). The negative direction confirms that words acquired earlier have a network of word associates that is more similar to those of adults, suggesting that convergence to adult semantic knowledge is at a more advanced state.

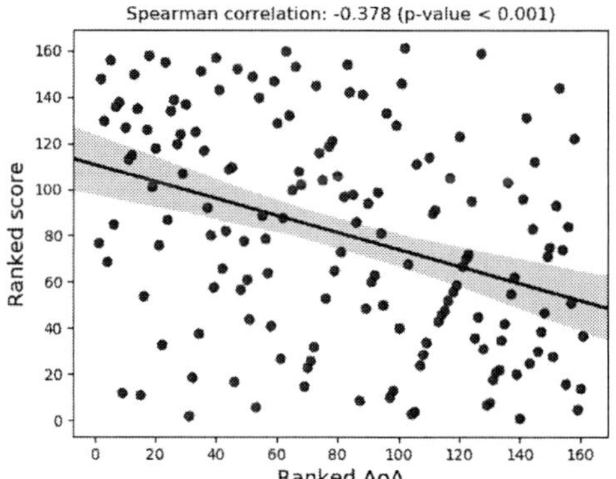

Figure 3: Ranked AoA and ranked score (number of overlaps), based on the 50 nearest neighbours in the best-performing model in the ND method.

One limitation of this procedure is that it requires a choice on the number of neighbours to be retrieved. In order to see how much the metric is affected by this parameter, we report the rank correlations of the previous model for several values of n. As can be seen in Figure 4, this number stabilizes after $n = 25$. The figure also shows whether this metric favours a model that did not perform well in our previous evaluation metric (SVD with window size 4, shift 15, frequency threshold 10). The graph shows that this model is consistently worse on our second evaluation method as well.

6   Conclusion

We proposed two methods to evaluate word embeddings for language acquisition. The main feature of these methods is the use of AoA norms for assessing whether the semantic organization of the word embeddings support the developmental trajectory of word learning.

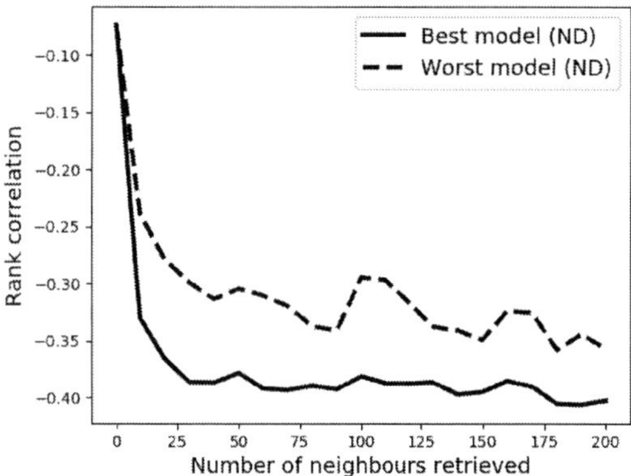

Figure 4: Rank correlations depending on the number of retrieved nearest neighbours, for the best and worst models in the previous evaluation method (ND).

The use of these metrics already prompted the discovery that (1) words with fewer neighbours are easier to acquire, suggesting competition of neighbouring words, and (2) at young age, infants only attend to very local context. The application of these methods to distributional models that incorporate additional assumptions (e.g. knowledge of word order) holds promise for further understanding of the role of distributional information in word learning.

References

Nicole Beckage, Linda Smith, and Thomas Hills. 2011. Small worlds and semantic network growth in typical and late talkers. *PloS One*, 6(5).

Simon De Deyne, Danielle J Navarro, Amy Perfors, Marc Brysbaert, and Gert Storms. 2019. The "small world of words" english word association norms for over 12,000 cue words. *Behavior research methods*, 51(3):987–1006.

Michael C Frank, Mika Braginsky, Daniel Yurovsky, and Virginia A Marchman. 2017. Wordbank: An open repository for developmental vocabulary data. *Journal of child language*, 44(3):677–694.

Thomas T Hills, Josita Maouene, Brian Riordan, and Linda B Smith. 2010. The associative structure of language: Contextual diversity in early word learning. *Journal of memory and language*, 63(3):259–273.

Omer Levy and Yoav Goldberg. 2014. Neural word embedding as implicit matrix factorization. In *Advances in neural information processing systems*, pages 2177–2185.

Omer Levy, Yoav Goldberg, and Ido Dagan. 2015. Improving distributional similarity with lessons learned from word embeddings. *Transactions of the Association for Computational Linguistics*, 3:211–225.

Brian MacWhinney. 2000. *The CHILDES Project: Transcription format and programs.* Lawrence Erlbaum Associates.

Tomas Mikolov, Ilya Sutskever, Kai Chen, Greg S Corrado, and Jeff Dean. 2013. Distributed representations of words and phrases and their compositionality. In *Advances in Neural Information processing systems*, pages 3111–3119.

Francisco Pereira, Samuel Gershman, Samuel Ritter, and Matthew Botvinick. 2016. A comparative evaluation of off-the-shelf distributed semantic representations for modelling behavioural data. *Cognitive neuropsychology*, 33(3-4):175–190.

Jenny R Saffran, Richard N Aslin, and Elissa L Newport. 1996. Statistical learning by 8-month-old infants. *Science*, 274(5294):1926–1928.

Alessandro Sanchez, Stephan C Meylan, Mika Braginsky, Kyle E MacDonald, Daniel Yurovsky, and Michael C Frank. 2019. childes-db: A flexible and reproducible interface to the child language data exchange system. *Behavior research methods*, 51(4):1928–1941.

Massimo Stella, Nicole M Beckage, and Markus Brede. 2017. Multiplex lexical networks reveal patterns in early word acquisition in children. *Scientific reports*, 7:46730.

Michael Tomasello, Sara Mannle, and Ann C Kruger. 1986. Linguistic environment of 1-to 2-year-old twins. *Developmental Psychology*, 22(2):169.

Guessing the Age of Acquisition of Italian Lemmas through Linear Regression

Irene Russo

Istituto di Linguistica Computazionale "Antonio Zampolli", Pisa
Via G. Moruzzi, 1, Pisa, Italy
`irene.russo@ilc.cnr.it`

Abstract

The age of acquisition of a word is a psycholinguistic variable concerning the age at which a word is typically learned. It correlates with other psycholinguistic variables such as familiarity, concreteness, and imageability. Existing datasets for multiple languages also include linguistic variables such as the length and the frequency of lemmas in different corpora.

There are substantial sets of normative values for English, but for other languages, such as Italian, the coverage is scarce. In this paper, a set of regression experiments investigates whether it is possible to guess the age of acquisition of Italian lemmas that have not been previously rated by humans. An intrinsic evaluation is proposed, correlating estimated Italian lemmas' AoA with English lemmas' AoA. An extrinsic evaluation - using AoA values as features for the classification of literary excerpts labeled by age appropriateness - shows how essential is lexical coverage for this task.

1 Introduction

The age of acquisition (AoA, henceforth) of a word as the age at which a word was typically learned is a well-know psycholinguistic variable investigated for multiple languages (Moors et al., 2013; Ferrand et al., 2008; Alonso et al., 2012). It correlates with other variables such as concreteness of a word, frequency in a corpus, length of the word in letters and syllables. AoA estimates can be obtained by asking parents to record data about their children while they grow up. They are more frequently obtained by requesting the experiment's participants to indicate at which age they learned different words.

The collection of such ratings in an experimental setting is time-consuming. For this reason, existing datasets tend to have low coverage. With the advent of crowdsourcing platforms, there have been multiple efforts to enlarge the lists of AoA estimates asking for words' ratings. Participants self-assessed the age (in years) at which they thought they had learned the word, meaning that they would have understood that word even if they would not have been able to use, read, or write it. Crowdsourced AoA estimates show a good correlation with analogous ratings from traditional experimental settings, validating this methodology to improve AoA lists' coverage in less time (Kuperman et al., 2012).

For psycholinguists, the AoA of a word is a crucial variable in the selection process of the stimuli for lexical decision task experiments. Its correlation with other variables indicates that multiple factors should be taken into account when testing hypotheses involving lexical semantics, to ensure the right level of variability and complexity in the stimuli set.

These multiple factors correlated with AoA of a lemma make it possible to use a regression model to guess lemmas' AoA[1]. In this paper, a set of regression experiments investigates which features help to guess the age of acquisition of Italian lemmas that humans have not previously rated. An intrinsic evaluation is proposed, correlating estimated Italian lemmas' AoA with English lemmas' AoA, as proposed by (Montefinese et al., 2019) to test the generalizability of AoA ratings.

The extrinsic evaluation investigates if a list of AoA with better coverage could be beneficial for all those NLP tasks that classify or order texts according to their cognitive complexity, following the research hypotheses investigated for English (Xia et al., 2016; Vajjala and Meurers, 2014). More specifically, through a regression-as-classification approach, preliminary results on the role of AoA of lemmas for the classification of children's literature excerpts labeled with age appropriateness

---

[1]In lexicographic terms, this paper investigates the age of acquisition of a lemma since existing datasets record this feature for lemmatized word and not for their inflected forms.

43

Proceedings of the Workshop on Cognitive Modeling and Computational Linguistics, pages 43–48
Online Event, November 19, 2020. ©2020 Association for Computational Linguistics
https://doi.org/10.18653/v1/P17

information are proposed.

2   Related Works

Several studies analyze how to extract psycholinguistic variables with corpus-based methodologies, with the aim of testing if this kind of knowledge is implicitly contained in the language. One practical aim is to create larger datasets of psycholinguistic norms avoiding the time-consuming phase of collections involving participants.

The seminal work of (Bestgen and Vincze, 2012) proposes latent semantic analysis to estimate lexical norms of words, obtaining satisfactory results for concreteness, imagery, and valence but less good for arousal and dominance. The age of acquisition is not included among the variables.

Mandera et al. (2015) build a semantic similarity space and apply machine learning techniques to extrapolate existing ratings of previously unrated words for five psycholinguistic properties (age of acquisition, concreteness, arousal, dominance and valence). The results are encouraging in terms of correlation with human norms. For example, the Pearson correlation is 0.737 for the age of acquisition of words, meaning that words related to similar topics are more likely to be acquired around the same age. However, according to the authors, evaluating the results in a lexical decision task is not satisfactory from a psycholinguistic perspective. The methodology used may introduce artifacts to the data and produce results that could lead to different conclusions that would be reached based on human ratings.

Hollis and Westbury (2012) use principal component analysis to understand the semantic dimensions along which the skip-gram model organizes meaning, finding how many dimensions are correlated with a particular semantic and lexical variable among the ones relevant for psycholinguistic research. Their findings confirm that the age of acquisition is in some way encoded in the semantic vector representation for word meanings, but no predictive methodology to assign a value to unrated words is implemented.

Vankrunkelsven et al. (2018) compare a distributional semantic model derived from word co-occurrences and a word association based model (with data collected from human subjects) in predicting psycholinguistic properties of words that affect lexical processing for Dutch. Overall, the correlations show a better performance of the methodology implemented (kNN) when word association information is used. Among the variables, estimates for the age of acquisition display the lowest correlation, while affective variables such as valence and concreteness are clearly encoded in the semantic models tested.

3   Datasets

A short description of all the datasets used in the experiments reported in Section 3 is provided in this section.

Montefinese et al. (2019): this dataset contains ratings for 1,957 Italian content lemmas evaluated by 507 native Italian speakers recruited online. The stimuli were distributed over 20 lists containing 97–98 words each; each lemma was rated by 25 participants. The collected judgments are plausible because of strong internal reliability and a good correlation (Pearson r = 0.697) with translated English norms (Kuperman et al., 2012).

This dataset also contains information about the word length (i.e., number of characters), the word frequency from two different corpora (La Repubblica and ItWac), and the number of orthographic neighbors. Table 1 reports the composition of the norms in terms of parts of speech.

part of speech	#lemmas
noun	1494
adjective	311
verb	152

Table 1:   Composition of (Montefinese et al. 2019) Italian AoA norms.

Kuperman et al. (2012): this dataset - the biggest one available - is composed of 30,121 English words with AoA ratings obtained through crowdsourcing (e.g., through Amazon Mechanical Turk). The ratings are reliable as those obtained in laboratory conditions. In Table 2 its composition in terms of the parts of speech included in the Italian dataset (adverbs are excluded) is presented.

part of speech	#lemmas
noun	18825
adjective	7259
verb	3622

Table 2:   Composition of (Kuperman et. al 2012) English AoA norms.

megahr_it: this dataset contains concreteness and

imageability estimates for 77 languages obtained through cross-lingual transfer via word embeddings (Ljubešić et al., 2018). Concreteness refers to the degree to which a concept denoted by a word refers to a perceptible entity. Imageability is a psycholinguistic variable that indicates how well a word gives rise to a mental image or sensory experience. The Italian dataset contains 100,000 words, 53% of them occurring among the most frequent 30,000 lemmas in La Repubblica lemmas' frequency list.

La Repubblica lemmas' frequency list: this list contains frequencies of lemmas in La Repubblica corpus (Baroni et al., 2004) and it's one the source for frequencies information included in (Montefinese et al., 2019).[2]

Visual Genome lemmas' frequency list: the Visual Genome dataset (Krishna et al., 2017) is the largest dataset of image descriptions for English. It is composed of dense annotations of objects, attributes, and relationships between objects for 108K images. As a pre-processing step, the descriptions have been annotated with TreeTagger (Schmid, 1994) and extracted the list of lemmas ordered by frequency. Frequencies in Visual Genome are included as a feature in linear regression experiments for estimating AoA of Italian lemmas to counterbalance La Repubblica frequency list where abstract meanings are more frequent.

4 Experiments

The training set is a subset of the Italian AoA norms dataset (Montefinese et al., 2019) resulting from the intersection of all datasets that contain features used for the linear regression experiments. As a consequence, it is smaller than the original dataset (see Table 3.)

part of speech	#lemmas
noun	1161
adjective	211
verbs	536
total	1908

Table 3: Composition of the training set.

The following features are included in the training set:

- L: lenght of each lemma;

- f_rep: the natural logarithm of the written frequency of lemmas in "La Repubblica" corpus (Baroni et al., 2004);

- f_vg: the natural logarithm of the frequency of lemmas in the Visual Genome descriptions corpus, mapped onto Italian lemmas through Open Multilingual Wordnet's alignment (Krishna et al., 2017);

- concreteness: rating about the perceptibility of a concept denoted by a lemma, extracted from the mega_hr dataset (Ljubešić et al., 2018);

- imageability: rating about the strenght of sensory experience associated with a concept, extracted from the mega_hr dataset (Ljubešić et al., 2018).

A linear regression model is implemented and its performance is evaluated through 10-cross fold validation on the Italian norms training set. The results for different combination of features are reported in Table 4. The first column reports the mean standard error, a common evaluation measure for regression experiments. The second reports Pearson correlation between the estimated AoA and the real one, contained in (Montefinese et al., 2019)'s dataset. Concerning parts of speech, adjectives show the best correlation (0.61) while nouns are more problematic (0.55) and verbs are in between (r = 0.58)[3]. The all features combination is then applied to the

features	MSE	Pearson r
L + f_rep	-1.46	0.32
L + f_vg	-1.45	0.34
L + f_rep + f_vg	-1.37	0.45
conc + imag	-1.47	0.30
all features	-1.23	0.58

Table 4: MSE and Pearson correlation between real and estimated AoA of Italian lemmas.

evaluation of a list of 2,783 not previously rated lemmas obtained considering the most frequent 8,000 lemmas in La Repubblica corpus and providing for each of them the part of speech and the

---

[2]The list is available at `wacky.sslmit.unibo.it`

[3]All the correlations reported in this paper are significant at the 0.05 level.

features	Pearson r
L + f_rep	0.242
L + f_vg	0.578
L + f_rep + f_vg	0.592
conc + imag	0.190
all features	0.515

Table 5: Pearson correlation between real English and estimated AoA of aligned Italian lemmas.

English translation found in the Open Multilingual Wordnet (Bond and Paik, 2012).

The estimaed AoA ratings are evaluated through a comparison with the English ones provided by (Kuperman et al., 2012). This comparison represents an intrinsic evaluation of the models since Pearson correlation between Italian and English AoA lemmas has been used by (Montefinese et al., 2019) to validate the generalizability of the collected norms. The correlation reported by the authors was 0.697. Table 5 reports the performance for new lemmas in terms of Pearson correlation with English lemmas. The best performance is achieved for verbs (0.646), then nouns (0.584) and adjectives (0.543). Surprisingly, the best result is not obtained with all features but with a combination of frequencies (from La Repubblica corpus and from the Visual Genome dataset) plus the length (i.e. number of character) of the lemmas.

5 Evaluation

The lists of 2,783 Italian lemmas with estimated AoA produced as a result of the linear regressions experiment presented in Section 3 can be evaluated on a dedicated dataset in a regression-as-classification task. A dataset of children's literature short texts is created, composed by epub excerpts made available by publishing houses[4]. From an e-commerce website[5] the appropriate age of potential readers is crawled.

The dataset is composed by 629 extracts (458,210 tokens in total, mean of each extract 728 tokens). Table 6 reports the composition of the children's literature excerpts corpus.

The set of features used for regression-as-classification experiments are based on the age of acquisition of lemmas:

- aoa_sum: sum of the age of acquisition values for rated lemmas as attested in texts;

[4] www.medialibrary.it
[5] www.ibs.it

features	excerpts
from 8 years	116
from 9 years	113
from 10 years	237
from 11 years	163

Table 6: Children's literature corpus, excerpts labeled by age appropriateness.

features	accuracy
set 1	0.372
set 2	0.354
set 3	0.325
set 4	0.348
set 1 + set 3	0.335
set 1 + set 4	0.330

Table 7: Pearson correlation between real and estimated age appropriateness of literary excerpts.

- aoa_mean: mean of the age of acquisition values in each text;

- aoa_std: standard deviation of the age of acquisition values in each text;

- aoa_max_value: maximum age of acquisition value occurring in a text;

- aoa_min_value: minimum age of acquisition value occurring in a text;

- max-min: difference between maximum and minimum age of acquisition values occurring in a text;

- frequency of occurrences from one to fourteen (set 2): number of occurrences of lemmas belonging to each age in the text;

- normalized frequency of occurrences from one to fourteen (set 3): number of occurrences of lemmas belonging to each age in the text, normalised by the total number of retrieved lemmas for each text;

- sum of all values from one to fourteen (set 4): sum of all values of lemmas belonging to each age in the text.

The best combination of features was found experimenting with (Montefinese et al., 2019)'s dataset, considering accuracy after rounding the linear regression outputs. In Table 7, the first six features constitute set 1.

features	accuracy
L + f_rep	0.378
L + f_vg	0.376
L + f_rep + f_vg	0.383
conc + imag	0.364
all features	0.379

Table 8: Pearson correlation between real and estimated age appropriateness of literary excerpts.

Since the best accuracy is obtained with features from set 1, the same set of features is applied for the evaluation of five AoA lists. Each list contains estimated AoA obtained with different set of features, as explained in Section 3. The aim is to test whether increasing the coverage of the Italian AoA dataset has positive effect on the classification of short texts by age appropriateness.

In line with what has been discovered about the correlation between English and Italian AoA values, the best set of features includes the frequencies from the two corpora and the lenght of the lemmas (see Table 8). Increasing (Montefinese et al., 2019)'s dataset with 2,783 lemmas with AoA estimated automatically slightly improves the accuracy in this specific classification task.

6 Conclusions and Future Works

In this paper, a set of regression experiments investigates if it is possible to guess the age of acquisition of Italian lemmas that humans have not previously rated by humans.

An intrinsic and extrinsic evaluation of the output is proposed. The results show that the overall quality of the estimated ratings enables their inclusion in NLP systems, even if they would not probably be satisfying for psycholinguistic experiments. More specifically, increasing the coverage of lexical resources containing AoA is beneficial for age appropriateness text classification.

As future work, the testing of semantic models for estimating the age of acquisition of Italian lemmas is relevant. Since the difficulty of a text could be assessed taking into account psycholinguistic variables that influence the cognitive complexity of the reading process, another interesting working hypothesis concerns the use of AoA features in other experiments involving the complexity of texts, such as readability assessment, L2 learners' written production, automatic assessment of text fluency for natural language generation outputs' evaluation.

References

María Angeles Alonso, Angel Fernandez, and Emiliano Díez. 2012. Subjective age-of-acquisition norms for 7,039 spanish words. *Behavior Research Methods*, (47):268–274.

Marco Baroni, Silvia Bernardini, Federica Comastri, Lorenzo Piccioni, Alessandra Volpi, Guy Aston, and Marco Mazzoleni. 2004. Introducing the la repubblica corpus: A large, annotated, TEI(XML)-compliant corpus of newspaper italian. In *Proceedings of the Fourth International Conference on Language Resources and Evaluation (LREC'04)*, Lisbon, Portugal. European Language Resources Association (ELRA).

Yves Bestgen and Nadja Vincze. 2012. Checking and bootstrapping lexical norms by means of word similarity indexes. *Behavior Research Methods*, (44):998–1006.

Francis Bond and Kyonghee Paik. 2012. A survey of wordnets and their licenses. In *Proceedings of the 6th Global WordNet Conference (GWC 2012)*.

Ludovic Ferrand, Patrick Bonin, Alain Méot, Maria Augustinova, Boris New, Christophe Pallier, and Marc Brysbaert. 2008. Age-of-acquisition and subjective frequency estimates for all generally known monosyllabic french words and their relation with other psycholinguistic variables. *Behavior Research Methods*, (40):1049–1054.

Geoff Hollis and Chris Westbury. 2012. The principals of meaning: Extracting semantic dimensions from co-occurrence models of semantics. *Psychonomic Bulletin Review*, (23):1744–1756.

Ranjay Krishna, Yuke Zhu, Oliver Groth, Justin Johnson, Kenji Hata, Joshua Kravitz, Stephanie Chen, Yannis Kalantidis, Li-Jia Li, David A. Shamma, Michael S. Bernstein, and Li Fei-Fei. 2017. Visual genome: Connecting language and vision using crowdsourced dense image annotations. *Int. J. Comput. Vision*, 123(1):32–73.

Victor Kuperman, Hans Stadthagen-Gonzalez, and Marc Brysbaert. 2012. Age-of-acquisition ratings for 30,000 english words. *Behavior Research Methods*, (44):978–990.

Nikola Ljubešić, Darja Fišer, and Anita Peti-Stantić. 2018. Predicting concreteness and imageability of words within and across languages via word embeddings. In *Proceedings of The Third Workshop on Representation Learning for NLP*, pages 217–222, Melbourne, Australia. Association for Computational Linguistics.

Paweł Mandera, Emmanuel Keuleers, and Marc Brysbaert. 2015. How useful are corpus-based methods for extrapolating psycholinguistic variables? *Quarterly journal of experimental psychology*, (68(8)):1623–1642.

Maria Montefinese, David Vinson, Gabriella Vigliocco, and Ettore Ambrosini. 2019. Italian age of acquisition norms for a large set of words (itaoa). *Frontiers in Psychology*, 10:278.

Agnes Moors, Jan De Houwer, Dirk Hermans, Sabine Wanmaker, Kevin van Schie, Anne-Laura Van Harmelen, Marteen De Schryver, Jeffrey De Winne, and Marc Brysbaert. 2013. Age-of-acquisition and subjective frequency estimates for all generally known monosyllabic french words and their relation with other psycholinguistic variables. *Behavior Research Methods*, (45):169–177.

Helmut Schmid. 1994. Probabilistic part-of-speech tagging using decision trees. In *Proceedings of International Conference on New Methods in Language Processing*.

Sowmya Vajjala and Detmar Meurers. 2014. Exploring measures of "readability" for spoken language: Analyzing linguistic features of subtitles to identify age-specific TV programs. In *Proceedings of the 3rd Workshop on Predicting and Improving Text Readability for Target Reader Populations (PITR)*, pages 21–29, Gothenburg, Sweden. Association for Computational Linguistics.

Steven Vankrunkelsven, Verheyen, Gert Storms, and Simon De Deyne. 2018. Predicting lexical norms: A comparison between a word association model and text-based word co-occurrence models. *Journal of Cognition*, (1(1)).

Menglin Xia, Ekaterina Kochmar, and Ted Briscoe. 2016. Text readability assessment for second language learners. In *Proceedings of the 11th Workshop on Innovative Use of NLP for Building Educational Applications*, pages 12–22, San Diego, CA. Association for Computational Linguistics.

Word Co-occurrence in Child-Directed Speech Predicts Children's Free Word Associations

Abdellah Fourtassi

Aix-Marseille Univ, Universite de Toulon, CNRS, LIS, ILCB, Marseille, France
abdellah.fourtassi@gmail.com

Abstract

The free association task has been very influential both in cognitive science and in computational linguistics. However, little research has been done to study how free associations develop in childhood. The current work focuses on the developmental hypothesis according to which free word associations emerge by mirroring the co-occurrence distribution of children's linguistic environment. I trained a distributional semantic model on a large corpus of child language and I tested if it could predict children's responses. The results largely supported the hypothesis: Co-occurrence-based similarity was a strong predictor of children's associative behavior even controlling for other possible predictors such as phonological similarity, word frequency, and word length. I discuss the findings in the light of theories of conceptual development.

1 Introduction

The mental lexicon is organized into a structure such that exposure to a given word, e.g. "cat", tends to activate semantically similar words such as "milk" or "dog" (Collins and Loftus, 1975; McNamara, 2005). In order to characterize this structure, researchers in cognitive science have often relied on the free association task where people are given a list of cue words and asked to provide the first words that come to mind. Data from this task — especially the word association norms collected by Nelson et al. (2004)— have proven successful in accounting for a variety of psycholinguistic phenomena (De Deyne and Storms, 2015). In addition, they have often been used as ground truth in evaluating the ability of NLP models to approximate human lexico-semantic organization (Silberer et al., 2013; Fourtassi and Dupoux, 2013; Vulić et al., 2017) .

While adult word associations have been extensively studied, it is still poorly understood how these associations develop in childhood. This is a significant gap in the developmental literature: To the extent that word free associations help us understand conceptual organization, the study of how these associations develop can inform our theories of conceptual development (Wojcik and Kandhadai, 2019).

Previous work has shown that adults' word associations can be predicted by patterns of co-occurrence in language use (Griffiths et al., 2007) (but see De Deyne et al. 2016), that is, pairs of words that tend to appear as cue-response in the free association data are also those that co-occur frequently in the language people are exposed to. Developmentally, thus, a plausible scenario is that word associations first originate in childhood by mirroring the co-occurrence distribution in the language children hear around them. Previous research has shown that word co-occurrence can support linguistic and conceptual development (e.g., Fourtassi et al. 2014, 2019), here I investigate how co-occurrence in child-directed speech can predict children's free associations.

The paper is organized as follows. First, I briefly present the data and methods. Second, I 1) quantify the variability in children's associations compared to that of adults, 2) explore if, despite individual variability, co-occurrence probabilities predict word associations, and 3) test if co-occurrence similarity remains predictive when controlling for other factors such as phonological similarity, response frequency, and response length. Finally, I discuss the results in the light of theories of early conceptual development.

2 Data and Methods

2.1 Word Association Data

I rely on a new dataset of children's free associations collected by Wojcik and Kandhadai (2019).

49

Proceedings of the Workshop on Cognitive Modeling and Computational Linguistics, pages 49–53
Online Event, November 19, 2020. ©2020 Association for Computational Linguistics
https://doi.org/10.18653/v1/P17

For a detailed description of the data collection process, please refer to that paper. In brief, the authors used age-appropriate stimuli to collect word associations from both children ($N = 60$; age range 3 – 8 years) and adults ($N = 60$). Participants were instructed to respond to a cue word with the first word that came to mind. The list of cue words consisted of 65 of the most frequent words in a large corpus of child language. It contained 25 nouns, 17 adjectives, 12 verbs, and 6 others (e.g., "yes").[1] Following Wojcik and Kandhadai (2019), and in order to maximize the statistical power of the analyses, participants were categorized by age group as "Adult", "Older children" (6 – 8 years), or "Younger children" (3–5 years).

2.2 Methods

2.2.1 Normalized Entropy

In order to quantify individual variability, I followed (Dubossarsky et al., 2017) in measuring, for each cue word y, the normalized entropy $H(y)$ defined as:

$$H(y) = \sum_{i=1}^{N} \frac{p(x_i) * log_2(p(x_i))}{log_2(N)}$$

Where $p(x_i)$ is the probability of a response x_i, which I obtain, for each cue y, by averaging across responses for that cue. N is the total number of different responses given by all participants for a given cue. H has values between 0 (total agreement) and 1 (no agreement).

2.2.2 Co-occurrence-based Similarity

I derived co-occurrence similarity in children's linguistic environment using Word2vec (Mikolov et al., 2013), a widely used distributional semantic model where pairs of words are assigned a similarity score based on the patterns of their co-occurrence in similar contexts (the context being the set of neighboring words). I trained the model on a large corpus of child language (CHILDES, MacWhinney 2000). Since I evaluate free association data of children aged 3 years and older, I chose to restrict the input data to the first three years (the common amount of exposure across age groups), allowing us to make comparison between age groups based on similar data. For comparison, I also used pre-trained vectors from Google

Freebase trained on about 100 billion words from various news articles.[2]

2.2.3 Phonological Distance

First, I converted the orthographic transcription of word pairs into their phonological forms using the CMU pronouncing dictionary. [3] Then, I measured the Levenshtein distance (also known as edit distance) of each pair. This measure counts the minimum number of operations (insertions, deletions, substitutions) required to change one member of the pair into the other. Based on previous research that reported children tend to give phonologically similar responses (e.g., "house" - "mouse") (Cronin, 2002), I defined a binary variable that distinguished between small values of edit distance (edit ≤ 1) and larger values (edit > 1).

2.2.4 Frequency and Length

Previous research has shown that both frequency and length play an important role in children's expressive language (Braginsky et al., 2019; Fourtassi et al., 2020). I test the extent to which they also constrain children's expressive free word associations. Note that while co-occurrence and phonological similarity characterize the relationship between the cue and the response, frequency and length characterize only the response: They capture possible response tendencies regardless of the identity of the cue word. I obtained word frequency based on CHILDES data and I defined word length as the number of phones in the phonological transcription.

3 Analyses

3.1 The Development of Individual Variability

In Figure 1, the normalized entropy by age group shows how heterogeneity in responses develops. Children had higher entropy than adults, showing a greater diversity in their responses. This result replicates findings by Wojcik and Kandhadai (2019) who used different measures such as idiosyncrasy (percent of responses given by only one participant) and the number of common responses. I did not find a difference between the younger and older children, however: Both had as much variability in their responses on average, suggesting that

---

[1] The data is publically available at osf.io/qat7w

[2] the pre-trained vectors can be found at https://code.google.com/archive/p/word2vec/

[3] Retrieved from http://www.speech.cs.cmu.edu/cgi-bin/cmudict

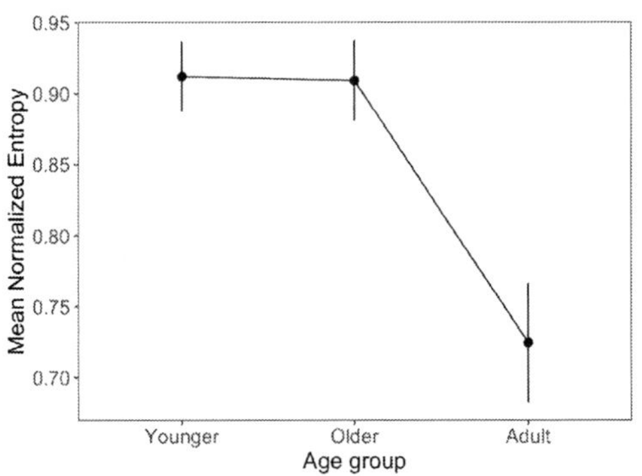

Figure 1: Mean normalized entropy by age group. The error bars indicate 95% confidence intervals.

children in this age range have not really started developing a shared lexical organization with one another, at least not to the same extent that adults do.

3.2 The Role of Co-occurrence in the Linguistic Environment

Figure 2 shows the average co-occurrence-based similarity of cue-response pairs in each age group using data from both CHILDES and Google Freebase. I found several interesting results. First, even Younger children were well above chance (chance being the average co-occurrence-based similarity between two random words), meaning that their associations already begins to reflect the co-occurrence distribution in the linguistic environment. Second, we see a clear developmental trend: On the one hand, older children had a higher correlation score than Younger children, suggesting that children mirror more and more the distribution of the input between 3 and 8 years old. On the other hand, adults had a higher score than older children, showing that development continues beyond this age range. Finally, I obtained similar developmental patterns whether I used CHILDES or Freebase, suggesting that children's associations reflect the distributional structure of their native language beyond the idiosyncrasies of child-directed speech.

3.3 Comparison to Other Developmental Factors

Here I examine how the role of co-occurrence compares to other possible predictors. I ran a mixed-effects model where the predicted variable was the probability of a response given a cue (obtained by summing over similar responses and dividing

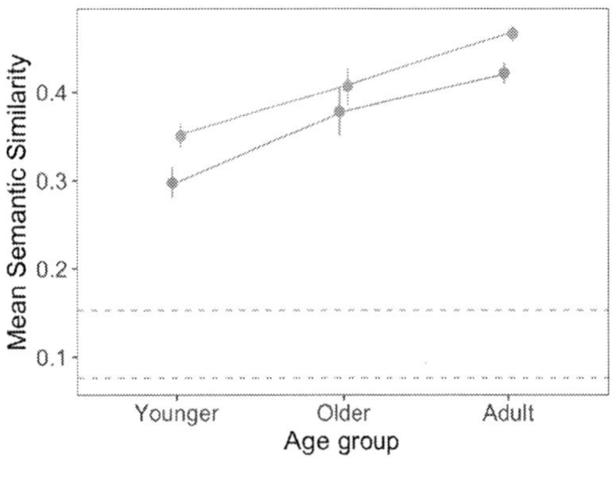

Figure 2: Average cosine similarity of cue-target pairs in each age group using data from both CHILDES and Freebase. The dotted lines represent chance similarity values in each training dataset. The error bars indicate 95% confidence intervals.

by all responses for a given cue). The predictors were the co-occurrence-based similarity from CHILDES (`co-occurrence`), phonological distance (`Phono`), log-frequency (`LogFreq`), and length (`Length`) (all were centered and scaled). To study change across time, I added an interaction term with age (`Age`) to each predictor. Finally, to take into account the possibly correlated data for the same cue, I specified `Cue` as a random effect in the model. The results of this regression are shown in Table 1.

Table 1: Estimates of a regression model predicting the probability of responses in free association data. The model was specified as `Response ~ (co-occurrence + Phono + LogFreq + Length)*Age + (1 | Cue)`

Predictors	Estimates (95% CI)
(Intercept)	7.997*** (6.497, 9.497)
Co-occurrence	4.562*** (3.924, 5.199)
LogFreq	2.022*** (1.314, 2.730)
Length	0.203 (−0.510, 0.916)
Phono	3.428*** (2.026, 4.831)
Age	−1.520 (−3.040, 0.0001)
Co-occurrence:Age	1.695*** (0.997, 2.393)
LogFreq:Age	1.004* (0.233, 1.774)
Length:Age	0.204 (−0.582, 0.989)
Phono:Age	2.045** (0.521, 3.570)
Note:	*p<0.05; **p<0.01; ***p<0.001

Confirming the previous analysis, the response's degree of co-occurrence with the cue strongly predicted the response's probability, even controlling for other predictors. The response's phonological distance with the cue and the response's frequency in the linguistic environment were also strong predictors of the response's probability. That is, participants were overall more likely to provide phonologically dissimilar and frequent responses. The length of the response, however, was not a significant predictor.

Concerning developmental change, co-occurrence strongly interacted with age, meaning that the effect of co-occurrence-based similarity becomes greater over development. The same can be said about phonological distance: Participants provide less and less phonologically similar response as they grow older. Frequency also varied with age, although to a lesser extent, meaning that responses get slightly more frequent over development.

in order to compare younger and older groups in a more direct fashion, I ran a second regression that was identical to the first one, but with adult data removed. In this second regression (estimates not shown here), co-occurrence-based similarity also interacted with age, indicating that a developmental change occurs between 3 and 8 years whereby children's responses mirror more and more the distribution of the language they are exposed to.

4   Discussion

Despite the fact that free associations varied greatly from child to child, they were highly predicted by their co-occurrence-based similarity in the linguistic environment. This prediction remained strong even controlling for other factors that may influence children's responses such as phonological similarity, word frequency, and word length. I found an interesting developmental change that appears to take place between 3 and 8 years old and whereby children's responses reflect more and more the co-occurrence structure of their native language, while becoming less tied to the lower-level phonological similarity. That said, I also found a difference between older children and adults, suggesting this development continues well into late childhood.

Since free associations have been used to study conceptual organization, the current study contributes to the literature on conceptual development. A big challenge in this literature is to understand how taxonomic categories (e.g., animal vs. artifact) are formed by children despite the fact that members of such categories do not necessarily look similar (e.g., fish and bird). Using free association data (the same I use here), Wojcik and Kandhadai (2019) showed that children's free associations become more paradigmatic/taxonomic in nature between 3 and 8 years old.

Researchers have suggested children can learn such abstract categories (at least partly) through the language they hear around them. In fact, cues from language can provide children with information beyond what they can obtain through observation alone (Gelman, 2009; Harris, 2012; Csibra and Gergely, 2009). In particular, word co-occurrence in child-directed speech has been shown to be a reliable cue for several taxonomic categories (Huebner and Willits, 2018; Fourtassi et al., 2019). For example, though "fish" and "bird" do not look very similar, people talk about them in similar linguistic contexts, typically leading to a high co-occurrence-based similarity.

The current study provides (correlational) evidence for this proposal by showing that, at the same time children's associations become more taxonomic (Wojcik and Kandhadai, 2019), they also become more tuned with the word co-occurrence distribution of their native language. I suggest that these are not totally independent developments, and more precisely, that the later could (at least partly) influence the former. If this were to be true, then we could possibly explain a major high-level episode in conceptual development based on a simple mechanism of tracking statistical co-occurrence in language (which we know children are highly skilled at, see Saffran et al. 1996).

Future investigations should go beyond the limitations of the current work. For example, here I predicted data from one set of children (free word association) with data about the experience of a completely different set (CHILDES corpus). Such a research approach has been used before (e.g., Braginsky et al. 2019). It is cost-effective, allowing us to collect large data and average out differences between children and their input. However, this approach fundamentally limits the amount of variability we can capture in terms of how the input may influence uptake. One way to mitigate this limitation is through doing dense data analysis, correlating input and behavior for the same child (e.g., Roy et al. 2015). Another (complementary) approach is to explore if the phenomenon can be produced in controlled, albeit simplified, behavioral experiments (e.g., Unger et al. 2020).

5 Acknowledgement

This research was supported by the grant ANR16-CONV-0002 (ILCB)

References

Mika Braginsky, Daniel Yurovsky, Virginia A Marchman, and Michael C Frank. 2019. Consistency and variability in children's word learning across languages. *Open Mind*, 3:52–67.

Allan M Collins and Elizabeth F Loftus. 1975. A spreading-activation theory of semantic processing. *Psychological review*, 82(6):407.

Virginia S Cronin. 2002. The syntagmatic-paradigmatic shift and reading development. *Journal of Child Language*, 29(1):189.

Gergely Csibra and György Gergely. 2009. Natural pedagogy. *Trends in cognitive sciences*, 13(4).

Simon De Deyne, Amy Perfors, and Daniel J Navarro. 2016. Predicting human similarity judgments with distributional models: The value of word associations. In *Proceedings of COLING 2016, the 26th International Conference on Computational Linguistics: Technical Papers*, pages 1861–1870.

Simon De Deyne and Gert Storms. 2015. Word associations. In *The Oxford Handbook of the Word*.

Haim Dubossarsky, Simon De Deyne, and Thomas T Hills. 2017. Quantifying the structure of free association networks across the life span. *Developmental psychology*, 53(8):1560.

Abdellah Fourtassi, Yuan Bian, and Michael C Frank. 2020. The growth of children's semantic and phonological networks: Insight from 10 languages. *Cognitive Science*, 44(7).

Abdellah Fourtassi, Ewan Dunbar, and Emmanuel Dupoux. 2014. Self-consistency as an inductive bias in early language acquisition. In *Proceedings of the Annual Meeting of the Cognitive Science Society*, volume 36.

Abdellah Fourtassi and Emmanuel Dupoux. 2013. A corpus-based evaluation method for distributional semantic models. In *51st Annual Meeting of the Association for Computational Linguistics Proceedings of the Student Research Workshop*, pages 165–171, Sofia, Bulgaria. Association for Computational Linguistics.

Abdellah Fourtassi, Isaac Scheinfeld, and Michael C Frank. 2019. The development of abstract concepts in children's early lexical networks. In *Proceedings of the Workshop on Cognitive Modeling and Computational Linguistics*, pages 129–133.

Susan A Gelman. 2009. Learning from others: Children's construction of concepts. *Annual review of psychology*, 60.

Thomas L Griffiths, Mark Steyvers, and Joshua B Tenenbaum. 2007. Topics in semantic representation. *Psychological review*, 114(2):211.

Paul L Harris. 2012. *Trusting what you're told: How children learn from others.* Harvard University Press.

Philip A Huebner and Jon A Willits. 2018. Structured semantic knowledge can emerge automatically from predicting word sequences in child-directed speech. *Frontiers in Psychology*, 9:133.

Brian MacWhinney. 2000. *The CHILDES Project: Tools for analyzing talk. transcription format and programs*, volume 1. Psychology Press.

Timothy P McNamara. 2005. *Semantic priming: Perspectives from memory and word recognition.* Psychology Press.

Tomas Mikolov, Ilya Sutskever, Kai Chen, Greg S Corrado, and Jeff Dean. 2013. Distributed representations of words and phrases and their compositionality. In *Advances in neural information processing systems*, pages 3111–3119.

Douglas L Nelson, Cathy L McEvoy, and Thomas A Schreiber. 2004. The university of south florida free association, rhyme, and word fragment norms. *Behavior Research Methods, Instruments, & Computers*, 36(3):402–407.

Brandon C Roy, Michael C Frank, Philip DeCamp, Matthew Miller, and Deb Roy. 2015. Predicting the birth of a spoken word. *Proceedings of the National Academy of Sciences*, 112(41):12663–12668.

Jenny R Saffran, Richard N Aslin, and Elissa L Newport. 1996. Statistical learning by 8-month-old infants. *Science*, 274(5294):1926–1928.

Carina Silberer, Vittorio Ferrari, and Mirella Lapata. 2013. Models of semantic representation with visual attributes. In *Proceedings of the 51st Annual Meeting of the Association for Computational Linguistics (Volume 1: Long Papers)*, pages 572–582, Sofia, Bulgaria. Association for Computational Linguistics.

Layla Unger, Olivera Savic, and Vladimir M Sloutsky. 2020. Statistical regularities shape semantic organization throughout development. *Cognition*, 198:104190.

Ivan Vulić, Douwe Kiela, and Anna Korhonen. 2017. Evaluation by association: A systematic study of quantitative word association evaluation. In *Proceedings of the 15th Conference of the European Chapter of the Association for Computational Linguistics: Volume 1, Long Papers*, pages 163–175.

Erica H Wojcik and Padmapriya Kandhadai. 2019. Paradigmatic associations and individual variability in early lexical–semantic networks: Evidence from a free association task. *Developmental Psychology*.

Development of Multi-level Linguistic Alignment in Child-Adult Conversations

Thomas Misiek   **Benoit Favre**   **Abdellah Fourtassi**

Aix-Marseille Univ, Universite de Toulon, CNRS, LIS, ILCB, Marseille, France

{thomas.misiek, benoit.favre, abdellah.fourtassi}@lis-lab.fr

Abstract

Interactive alignment is a major mechanism of linguistic coordination. Here we study the way this mechanism emerges in development across the lexical, syntactic, and conceptual levels. We leverage NLP tools to analyze a large-scale corpus of child-adult conversations between 2 and 5 years old. We found that, across development, children align consistently to adults above chance and that adults align consistently more to children than vice versa (even controlling for language production abilities). Besides these consistencies, we found a diversity of developmental trajectories across linguistic levels. These corpus-based findings provide strong support for an early onset of multi-level linguistic alignment in children and invite new experimental work.

1   Introduction

Linguistic alignment is the tendency that interlocutors have to change the way they talk to accommodate their conversational partners. This can happen through mirroring the partner's linguistic behavior on many levels such as the choice of words, syntactic structures, and semantic topics. Linguistic alignment is considered an important mechanism for establishing common ground and rapport, fostering successful communicative interactions (Clark, 1996) . In addition, understanding this coordination in its natural context is crucial for the design of conversational systems that interact with people in a natural and effective fashion (Zhao et al., 2016; Loth et al., 2015; Park et al., 2017).

While alignment has been largely studied with adults (Pickering and Garrod, 2004; Fusaroli et al., 2012; Dale et al., 2013; Doyle and Frank, 2016; Dideriksen et al., 2019), little has been done to investigate how it manifests in the context of child-adult early communication and how it evolves across development. This is a significant gap in the literature. The child-adult early communication cannot be thought of as a simple extension of conversational dynamics between adults; it involves strong asymmetries in terms of cognitive abilities and social roles and, thus, requires more dedicated research (Clark, 2015). In addition, the study of child-caregiver linguistic interaction informs our theories of children's cognitive development. On the one hand, children's developing abilities in managing a conversation — through mechanisms such as interactive alignment — is a window into their emerging social-cognitive skills (Tomasello, 2009). On the other hand, the way caregivers use alignment across development allows us to understand whether and how adults tune their talk to children's developing cognitive abilities. Such tuning has been suggested to play a pedagogical role, supporting linguistic and conceptual learning (Snow, 1972; Fourtassi et al., 2014, 2019).

Related Work and Novelty of the Current Study

Our study investigates children's interactive alignment in natural conversations with adults. Previously, Dale and Spivey (2006) used recurrence analysis to investigate child-caregiver syntactic alignment (operationalized as sequences of parts of speech) and found evidence for syntactic coordination. Using a similar computational framework, Fernández and Grimm (2014) extended Dale and Spivey's findings to the lexical and conceptual levels. Nevertheless, both studies were based on data from three children only. While such a small sample size allows for a detailed examination of development for specific children, it does not allow us to characterize general developmental patterns that could be shared by the majority of children. Indeed, both studies found large individual variability and, thus, no strong conclusions about development could be drawn.

Proceedings of the Workshop on Cognitive Modeling and Computational Linguistics, pages 54–58

Online Event, November 19, 2020. ©2020 Association for Computational Linguistics

https://doi.org/10.18653/v1/P17

In a more recent work, Yurovsky et al. (2016) studied a large-scale corpus of child-caregiver interactions containing two orders of magnitude more children than previous work. Using hierarchical Bayesian models, they found that both children and caregivers decreased their alignment over the first five years of development. Work by Yurovsky et al. (2016) thus provided a much more robust test of interactive alignment. However, it focused on the special case of function words. It is still an open question how development unfolds across the entire lexicon and along more abstract levels such as syntax and semantics. The current study is an effort to fill this gap in the literature. We leverage NLP tools to test interactive alignment at the lexical, syntactic, and conceptual levels, using a large-scale corpus of children's natural language.

2 Data and Methods

2.1 Data

Following Yurovsky et al. (2016), and in order to maximize the statistical power and generalizability of our analysis, we selected all English-language data available in CHILDES (MacWhinney, 2000) for children between 2 to 5 years; a time of rapid growth in terms of expressive language and social-cognitive skills (Wellman, 2014). This resulted in 5,152 total transcripts across 725 unique children. The number of transcripts per child varied between 1 ($N = 381$) and 503 ($N = 1$), with an average of about 7 transcripts per child.

2.2 Levels of Linguistic Alignment

We study linguistic alignment, on a turn-by-turn basis. We measure alignment along the lexical, syntactic, and conceptual level, following largely operationalizations in Fernández and Grimm (2014).

Lexical Alignment

Lexical alignment characterizes the speaker's reuse of words from the interlocutor's previous utterance. We captured this phenomenon by counting the number of shared ngrams (unigrams, bigrams and trigrams) across pairs of turns, normalized by the number of all possible ngrams.

Syntactic Alignment

Syntactic alignment was approximated by measuring the extent to which the speaker re-uses Part of Speech (PoS) ngrams from the interlocutor's previous utterance. In order to disentangle syntactic from lexical measures, we only took into account the PoS ngrams where at least one word was not identical. We counted the number of shared PoS ngrams (bigrams and trigrams) across pairs of turns, normalized by the number of all possible ngrams. The PoS tags in CHILDES were automatically generated using the Morphological Analysis algorithm (MOR, MacWhinney 2000) which yields a high accuracy rate on CHILDES adult data (above 99%).

Conceptual Alignment

Conceptual alignment aims at quantifying the degree to which interlocutors talk about conceptually similar things, without necessarily using similar words or syntactic structures. We computed this similarity as follows. First, we represented the utterances with vectors in a high dimensional space. These vectors were constructed by adding up the vectors corresponding to the content words present in the utterance. One way to obtain word vectors is by training a distributional semantic model on CHILDES data. However, since we are not studying semantic similarity from the perspective of the child, there is a priori no reason to limit training only to the children's surrounding language. Instead, we used vectors that were pre-trained on a much larger corpus than CHILDES, leading to a more robust similarity space. We used word2vec vectors (Mikolov et al., 2013) pre-trained on part of Google News dataset (about 100 billion words).[1] Second, we computed the standard cosine similarity between pairs of utterances' vectors. In order to disentangle conceptual from lexical similarity, we only computed the similarity between turns with no lexical overlap.

2.3 Types of Interactive Alignment

All our measures of alignment were normalized, taking values between 0 (absence of alignment) and 1 (identical repetition). Investigation of data across all measures showed that only conceptual alignment approximated a normal distribution. In contrast, both lexical and syntactic alignment data had an exceeding number of zeros and (to a lesser extent) ones. If the zeros and ones are removed, the data approximate a normal distribution. A similar phenomenon (especially zero-inflation) has previously been documented with adult-adult alignment data as well (Dideriksen et al., 2019).

There is no simple parametric distribution that can capture simultaneously the three modes of the

---

[1] We obtained these vectors from: https://code.google.com/archive/p/word2vec/

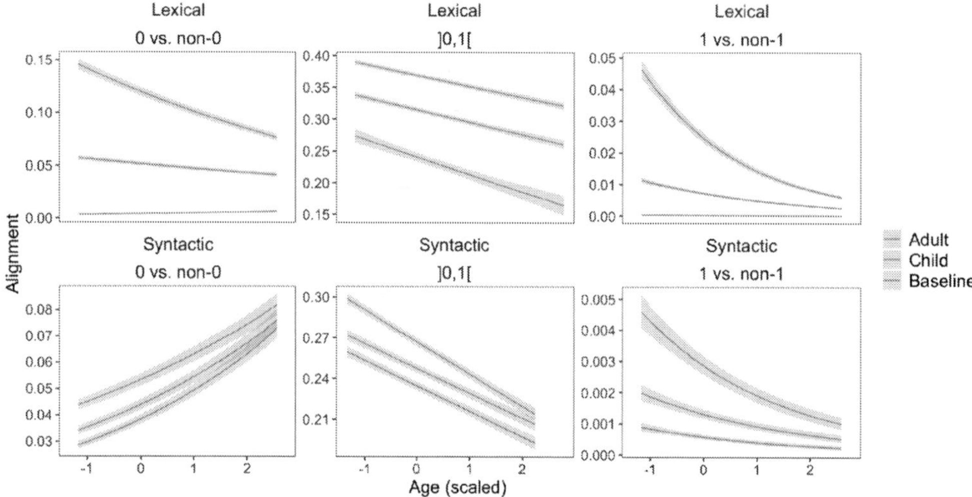

Figure 1: Changes in alignment across linguistic levels and alignment types for children between 2 and 5 years old (age was scaled). Data show the marginal effect of age by direction (Adults aligning to children or vice versa) as well as a baseline representing alignment between randomly selected pairs of child-adult turns from the same conversation/transcript. Ranges represent 95% confidence intervals. Here we show the results for the bigram-based measures only. The patterns were similar for the unigram- and trigram-based measures.

distribution. They are better analyzed in terms of three separate statistical processes (see Ospina and Ferrari 2012), which map on, conceptually, to three types of alignment. The first is a binary process that determines the presence or absence of alignment (i.e., 0 vs. non-0). This process maps on to the propensity to align at all. The second is a continuous process that determines the degree of alignment when this alignment is partial (i.e., with values in the open interval]0,1[). Such a measure allows us to characterize how alignment is used to manage a conversation: the speaker creates rapport by borrowing some words and structures form their interlocutor, while keeping the conversation going by adding new information. Finally, a binary process that determines total overlap as opposed to partial or zero overlap (i.e., 1 vs. non-1). This process maps on to the tendency to repeat the exact utterance (at least for the lexical measure). This type of alignment may play a different communicative role than partial alignment (e.g., echolalia in children with autism).

Critically, these phenomena may not follow the same developmental trajectory. For instance, it is possible that the propensity to alignment increases over development while the degree of this alignment decreases, or vice versa. Besides, both propensity and degree of alignment may be independent of the tendency to repeat the interlocutor's utterances.

3   Analyses and Discussion

We model each type of alignment with a separate mixed-effects model, predicting alignment at a given linguistic level (lexical, syntactic, and conceptual) by age and alignment direction (Adults aligning to children or vice versa). To take into account possibly correlated data from the same child, we used the identity of the child as a random effect.[2] For the binary processes (i.e., 0 vs. non-0 and 1 vs. non-1), the model was fit using binomial regressions. For the continuous process (i.e.,]0,1[), the model was fit using a linear regression. Figures 1 and 2 show the results.

Children Align Consistently

Children's alignment to adults was above the baseline (defined as alignment between randomly selected pairs of utterances in the same conversation) and this above-random alignment was consistent across development. This result was strikingly robust across all linguistic levels and alignment types, thus providing the strongest evidence to date about young children's abilities to engage in multi-level interactive alignment from as early as two years old.

---

[2]The model was specified as follows: Measure $\sim$ Age * Direction + (1 | child)

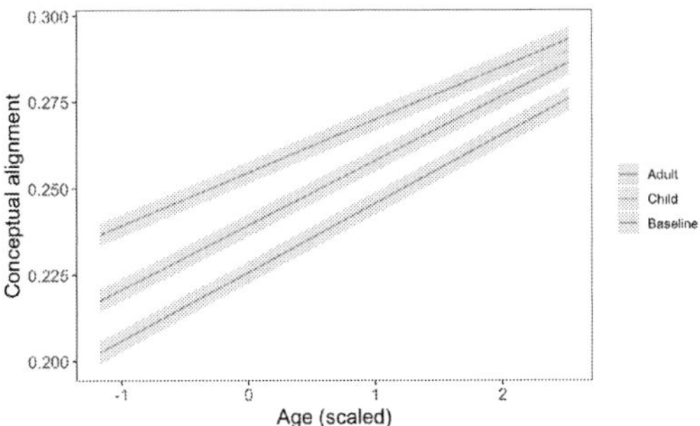

Figure 2: Changes in alignment at the conceptual level for children between 2 and 5 years old (age was scaled). Data show the marginal effect of age by direction. Ranges represent 95% confidence intervals.

Adults Align More

Another result — that was equally robust — is the fact that adults aligned more to children than children did to adults. Could this asymmetry in alignment be simply explained by the asymmetry in terms of language production abilities? Indeed, young children's ability to align will naturally be hindered if caregivers utter words that these children do not yet know or produce. We tested this hypothesis as follows.

First, we counted, for every pair of turns, the number of words uttered by the adult that the child may not know, which we determined roughly based on whether or not this word occurs in the sum of all children's production by that age/month in our corpus.[3] Second, we ran different mixed effect models where, in an addition to age and direction as predictors (as in the original modeling), we add the proportion of unknown words by children. All models (7 in total) showed a significant effect of alignment direction, suggesting that child-caregiver alignment asymmetry reflects genuine differences in conversational strategies beyond mere language production abilities (at least as quantified by our rough measure of word knowledge).

Development Across Linguistic Levels

For the lexical measure, which reflects alignment at the surface form, we found a declining trend across the board. Both children and adults use less exact words from their interlocutors as children develop. This result validates the finding of Yurovsky et al. (2016) and extends it beyond function words. As for the syntactic and conceptual measures, which reflect alignment at a more abstract level,[4] we found evidence for an increase in alignment (but only in the propensity to alignment for syntax). Interestingly though, in both cases we observe a similar increase in the random baseline, suggesting that this development likely reflects general enrichment in children's expressive language, rather than changes in their local conversational strategies. For example, if children start using more function words in their production, this would create more opportunity for syntactic alignment both locally (between adjacent turns) and globally (between random turns, i.e., the baseline). Similarly, if children start using more semantically specific words, relating to the topic of the discussion, this would increase conceptual similarity both between adjacent turns and (to a lesser extent) between more distant ones.

Development Across Alignment Types

The three alignment types did not follow a similar developmental trajectory. For example, we observed a clear dissociation in syntax between the general propensity to align (which increases) and the degree of alignment (which decreases). The tendency to repeat the structure of the entire utterance is the type of alignment where we found the largest difference in development between children and adults. While this tendency did not change much for children, it started relatively high with adults and almost converged with children's level by 5 years old.

4 Conclusion and Future Work

This study offered the first large-scale test to multi-level alignment in the context of natural child language. The results confirm some previous findings and uncover new ones. One question for future experimental work is whether such patterns can be produced in controlled behavioral experiments. Finally, while we addressed English-speaking children's interactions, we plan to generalize this work cross-culturally in future investigations.

5 Acknowledgement

Research supported by ANR16-CONV-0002

---

[3]The standard way to quantify children's average age of word production is through the Communicative Development Inventory (CDI), but available CDI data only goes up to 3 years old.

[4]Remember that in both measures, we only used instances where there was no overlap with lexical alignment

References

Eve V. Clark. 2015. Common ground. In *The Handbook of Language Emergence*, pages 328–353.

Herbert H Clark. 1996. *Using language*. Cambridge university press.

Rick Dale, Riccardo Fusaroli, Nicholas D Duran, and Daniel C Richardson. 2013. The self-organization of human interaction. In *Psychology of learning and motivation*, volume 59, pages 43–95. Elsevier.

Rick Dale and Michael J Spivey. 2006. Unraveling the dyad: Using recurrence analysis to explore patterns of syntactic coordination between children and caregivers in conversation. *Language Learning*, 56(3):391–430.

Christina Dideriksen, Riccardo Fusaroli, Kristian Tylén, Mark Dingemanse, and Morten H Christiansen. 2019. Contextualizing conversational strategies: backchannel, repair and linguistic alignment in spontaneous and task-oriented conversations. In *CogSci'19*, pages 261–267.

Gabriel Doyle and Michael C Frank. 2016. Investigating the sources of linguistic alignment in conversation. In *Proceedings of the 54th Annual Meeting of the Association for Computational Linguistics (Volume 1: Long Papers)*, pages 526–536.

Raquel Fernández and Robert Grimm. 2014. Quantifying categorical and conceptual convergence in child-adult dialogue. In *Proceedings of the Annual Meeting of the Cognitive Science Society*, volume 36.

Abdellah Fourtassi, Ewan Dunbar, and Emmanuel Dupoux. 2014. Self-consistency as an inductive bias in early language acquisition. In *Proceedings of the Annual Meeting of the Cognitive Science Society*, volume 36.

Abdellah Fourtassi, Isaac Scheinfeld, and Michael C Frank. 2019. The development of abstract concepts in children's early lexical networks. In *Proceedings of the Workshop on Cognitive Modeling and Computational Linguistics*, pages 129–133.

Riccardo Fusaroli, Bahador Bahrami, Karsten Olsen, Andreas Roepstorff, Geraint Rees, Chris Frith, and Kristian Tylén. 2012. Coming to terms: Quantifying the benefits of linguistic coordination. *Psychological Science*, 23(8):931–939.

Sebastian Loth, Katharina Jettka, Manuel Giuliani, and Jan P De Ruiter. 2015. Ghost-in-the-machine reveals human social signals for human–robot interaction. *Frontiers in psychology*, 6:1641.

Brian MacWhinney. 2000. *The CHILDES Project: Tools for analyzing talk. transcription format and programs*, volume 1. Psychology Press.

Tomas Mikolov, Ilya Sutskever, Kai Chen, Greg S Corrado, and Jeff Dean. 2013. Distributed representations of words and phrases and their compositionality. In *Advances in neural information processing systems*, pages 3111–3119.

Raydonal Ospina and Silvia LP Ferrari. 2012. A general class of zero-or-one inflated beta regression models. *Computational Statistics & Data Analysis*, 56(6):1609–1623.

Hae Won Park, Mirko Gelsomini, Jin Joo Lee, and Cynthia Breazeal. 2017. Telling stories to robots: The effect of backchanneling on a child's storytelling. In *2017 12th ACM/IEEE International Conference on Human-Robot Interaction (HRI*, pages 100–108.

Martin J Pickering and Simon Garrod. 2004. Toward a mechanistic psychology of dialogue. *Behavioral and brain sciences*, 27(2):169–190.

Catherine E Snow. 1972. Mothers' speech to children learning language. *Child development*, pages 549–565.

Michael Tomasello. 2009. *The cultural origins of human cognition*. Harvard university press.

Henry M Wellman. 2014. *Making minds: How theory of mind develops*. Oxford University Press.

Daniel Yurovsky, Gabriel Doyle, and Michael C Frank. 2016. Linguistic input is tuned to children's developmental level. In *CogSci*.

Ran Zhao, Tanmay Sinha, Alan W Black, and Justine Cassell. 2016. Automatic recognition of conversational strategies in the service of a socially-aware dialog system. In *Proceedings of the 17th Annual Meeting of the Special Interest Group on Discourse and Dialogue*, pages 381–392.

Conditioning, but on which distribution?
Grammatical gender in German plural inflection

Kate McCurdy   Adam Lopez   Sharon Goldwater
Institute for Language, Cognition and Computation
School of Informatics
University of Edinburgh
`kate.mccurdy@ed.ac.uk`

Abstract

Grammatical gender is a consistent and informative cue to the plural class of German nouns. We find that neural encoder-decoder models learn to rely on this cue to predict plural class, but adult speakers are relatively insensitive to it. This suggests that the neural models are not an effective cognitive model of German plural formation.

1 Introduction

In recent years, neural models of natural language have proven to be powerful *statistical learners*, capable of representing linguistic patterns and the conditions under which they generalize to new forms (e.g. Kirov and Cotterell, 2018). Artificial language learning experiments show that humans are also statistical learners: when patterns appear consistently with certain cues in the input, speakers consistently rely on those cues to generalize patterns to new forms (Newport, 2016).

Our research examines how two different statistical learners — neural encoder-decoder (ED) models and adult German speakers — use the cue of grammatical gender in plural inflection of novel words. Gender has a high statistical association with plural suffix: the feminine noun *Wahl* ("vote") is *Wahlen* in the plural, but the rhyming neuter noun *Mal* ("time") has the plural form *Male*. We expect that both speakers and the ED model will produce distributions over plural forms which are heavily conditioned on the gender of the input word. We find that the neural model is highly sensitive to grammatical gender; however, speaker productions, while slightly influenced by gender, appear more consistent with a distribution over plural suffixes which is *unconditioned* on gender. This surprising result suggests that, even though gender is a very informative cue to plural class, speakers may preferentially attend to different cues.

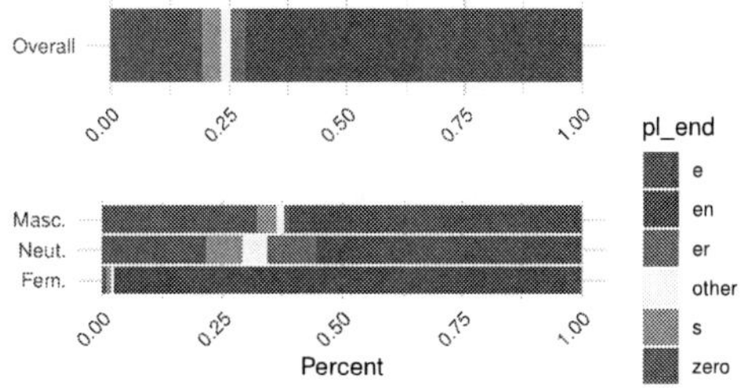

Figure 1: Distribution of plural suffix overall (upper) and by gender (lower) in the UniMorph corpus.

2 Background

German plural inflection is realized by five major suffixes, none of which commands a majority in either type or token frequency.[1] The two most frequent suffixes, -e and -(e)n, each apply to roughly 35-40% of German nouns (Figure 1, upper). With no majority class, how can a learner determine which pattern to generalize to new words?

One major cue to plural class comes from a noun's *grammatical gender*. The strong statistical association between grammatical gender and plural inflection class is widely recognized in the literature (Zaretsky et al., 2013; Yang, 2016; Williams et al., 2020, to cite some recent examples), and readily apparent in Figure 1 (lower), which shows the distribution of plural suffixes by noun gender in the UniMorph corpus (Kirov et al., 2016). Of the two most frequent plural suffixes, -(e)n is highly associated with feminine nouns, and -e with non-feminine (masculine and neuter); the tendency is so strong that some researchers have analyzed these suffixes as gender-conditioned "defaults" (Indefrey, 1999; Laaha et al., 2006). From this perspective, grammatical gender provides a highly consistent cue to plural class membership, which ought to inform a statistical learner's generalizations. Fur-

---

[1]For simplicity, this discussion focuses on suffixes and omits related phenomena such as umlaut.

Proceedings of the Workshop on Cognitive Modeling and Computational Linguistics, pages 59–65
Online Event, November 19, 2020. ©2020 Association for Computational Linguistics
https://doi.org/10.18653/v1/P17

thermore, grammatical gender is expressed on the article preceding a noun, and this initial position is perceptually salient to speakers (Frigo and McDonald, 1998). These properties suggest that grammatical gender should influence how speakers inflect novel nouns, and indeed, several *wug tests*[2] on German-speaking adults have found significant effects of gender (Köpcke 1988; Zaretsky and Lange 2016; though c.f. Marcus et al. 1995). Based on the artificial language learning literature (e.g. Newport, 2016), we might expect speakers to display *conditional probability matching* on novel German nouns, such that the probability of a noun taking a certain plural inflection — in particular, the two highly frequent classes -e and -(e)n — depends upon its grammatical gender.

Neural encoder-decoder (ED) models have recently been proposed for consideration as models of speaker cognition (Kirov and Cotterell, 2018). This has prompted investigation into the extent to which these models capture speaker behavior (Corkery et al., 2019; King et al., 2020; McCurdy et al., 2020). Earlier work suggests that neural models of German plural inflection are sensitive to grammatical gender: Goebel and Indefrey (2000) found that a simple recurrent network learned to favor -e plurals for masculine nouns, and -(e)n when the same nouns were presented as feminine gender. We hypothesize that neural models and adult speakers are equally capable of using the information available from grammatical gender to predict number inflection. We expect both to demonstrate similar gender-conditioned probability matching to the distribution shown in Figure 1 (lower), resulting in a majority use of -(e)n for feminine nouns, and -e for masculine and neuter nouns.

3 Method

To compare how grammatical gender influences plural inflection for German speakers and neural models, we use a parallel production task on nonce words (a wug test) for both speakers and model. Our study largely follows the data collection and modeling procedures of McCurdy et al. (2020).

Stimuli We use the 24 made-up nouns developed by Marcus et al. (1995), listed in Appendix A. By design, these nouns lack strong phonological cues

to plural class.[3] In their original study, Marcus et al. did not find a significant effect of grammatical gender; however, Zaretsky and Lange (2016) used the same stimuli and reported gender effects in the expected direction — participants used -(e)n more on feminine nouns, and -e more for nonfeminine nouns. Zaretsky and Lange speculate that these discrepant findings stem from differences in the two study designs: scale (the earlier study had 48 participants, the later one 585) and task (acceptability ratings vs. elicited productions). A third differentiating factor is the presence of semantic cues in the Marcus et al. study, which provided sentence contexts around the nonce words; for example, a sentence like *Die grünen BRALS sind billiger* ("The green brals are cheaper") would imply that the nonce word *Bral* referred to an object, whereas *Die BRALS sind ein bißchen komisch* ("The Brals are a bit weird") would imply that *Bral* was a family name. As adult learners can attend to formal and semantic cues under different conditions (Culbertson et al., 2017), it's possible that this manipulation directed participant focus toward semantic cues rather than grammatical gender. Zaretsky and Lange provided no semantic context in their experiment, only presenting the indefinite article and word form to participants (e.g. *Ein Bral*, "a [masculine/neuter] bral"). Our experimental design for both speakers and the neural model is closer to that of Zaretsky and Lange (2016): we elicit plural form productions and provide no semantic cues. This suggests we might also expect to find a robust effect of grammatical gender for these stimuli.

Human data collection We collected production data from 92 native German speakers[4] through an online survey. Participants saw each noun in the singular with a definite article indicating grammatical gender (e.g. *Der Bral* for masculine, *Das Bral* neuter, *Die Bral* feminine), and typed a plural-inflected form. Participants were randomly assigned to one of three lists. Grammatical gender was counterbalanced within lists (each participant saw 8 feminine, 8 masculine, and 8 neuter nouns) and across lists (each noun appeared with a different gender in each list).

---

[2]A wug test is the task of inflecting an novel word (e.g. "wug" in English). This task lets researchers observe which inflectional variants speakers use (e.g plural "wugs"; Berko, 1958).

[3]Certain phones in word-final position are highly associated with specific plural suffixes. The most consistent associations are found with vowels: words ending in schwa generally take -(e)n, and words ending in full vowels generally take -s (MacWhinney, 1978). Our stimuli all have word-final consonants, which lack strong associations with plural class.

[4]Participants were recruited through the platform Prolific. Of 100 tested, 8 were excluded for failing attention checks.

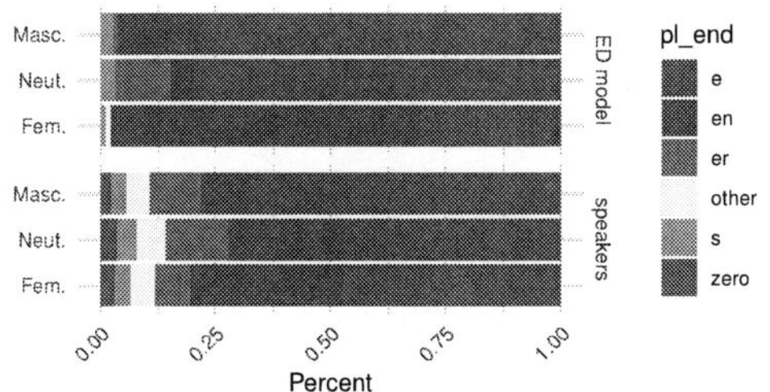

Figure 2: Plural suffix productions by gender, speakers (lower) vs. ED model (upper)

	Overall-TF	Gender-TF	ED
Speakers	**.67**	.49	.49
	(.60, .72)	(.40, .56)	(.35, .61)
ED	.41	**.62**	
	(.27, .54)	(.50, .71)	

Table 1: Correlations (Pearson's *r*, 95% confidence intervals in parentheses below) between item-level production percentages for speakers and ED model with 1) overall type frequency (Overall-TF), 2) gender-conditioned type frequency (Gender-TF), 3) each other.

Encoder-decoder model A neural encoder-decoder (ED) model encodes an input sequence into a fixed vector representation and then incrementally decodes it into a corresponding output sequence (Sutskever et al., 2014). We follow other recent work in using the architecture of Kann and Schütze (2016), which has been proposed for cognitive modeling (Kirov and Cotterell, 2018).

For the task of German number inflection, the ED takes as input a character sequence representing the singular nominative form of a noun, preceded by a special character for grammatical gender (e.g. ⟨*f*⟩ W A H L; ⟨*f*⟩ indicates feminine, ⟨*m*⟩ masculine, and ⟨*n*⟩ neuter). The model is trained to produce the noun's corresponding nominative plural form as output (e.g. W A H L E N). We used the 11,243 German nouns in UniMorph (Kirov et al., 2016) as our corpus, and added noun gender by merging the dataset with another Wiktionary scrape.[5] We follow the modeling procedure of McCurdy et al. (2020), who found that neural ED models correctly learned the most frequent plural suffix for neuter stimuli, but did not evaluate sensitivity to grammatical gender; please see their paper for further implementation details.

Following Corkery et al. (2019), we trained 25 separate random initializations of the same model architecture. This allows separate model instances to be treated as simulated "speakers", letting us aggregate productions and compare more directly to human speaker data. For evaluation, we combined each of the 24 noun stimuli with each of the three grammatical genders, and provided the resulting 72 items as input to each model instance.

4 Results

Our results (Figure 2) show that both speakers and the ED model are sensitive to grammatical gen-

der, but the model relies on this cue considerably more than speakers. Statistical analysis confirms that a) both speakers and the model show reliable effects of grammatical gender on their plural form productions, and b) gender effects are substantially greater for model productions. We fit two logistic mixed-effects models to separately analyze production of -e and -(e)n. Details of our analysis can be found in Appendix B. For both suffixes, we found a significant main effect of gender, and a significant interaction with data source, indicating that gender effects were amplified by the model.

Intriguingly, the speaker productions are not only less sensitive to grammatical gender, they also appear very consistent with the overall type frequency distribution of the plural suffixes, *unconditioned* on gender. To quantify this intuition, we looked at how the distribution of plural suffixes produced over each of the 72 noun-gender item combinations *correlated* to various other metrics. We asked three questions: 1) How well do item-level speaker and ED model productions correlate with *each other*? 2) How well do both sets of item-level productions correlate with the *gender-conditioned distribution* of plural suffix types observed in the German lexicon? 3) How well do both sets correlate with the *unconditioned overall distribution* of types? Table 1 shows the results: while item-level ED outputs are most correlated with the gender-conditioned distribution, item-level speaker data is most correlated[6] with the overall (unconditioned) type frequency.[7] Even though the speaker and ED data are matched by item, their productions have a lower correlation with each other than with the general type-frequency distributions.

[5] https://github.com/gambolputty/german-nouns/

---

[6] Table 1 shows results from Pearson's linear correlation; analysis with Spearman's rank correlation coefficient showed the same trend.

[7] To avoid potential confounds from both training and measuring on the UniMorph corpus, our estimates of gender-conditioned and overall type frequency are derived from Zaretsky et al. (2013)'s analysis of the thousand most frequent nouns from the DeReWo corpus.

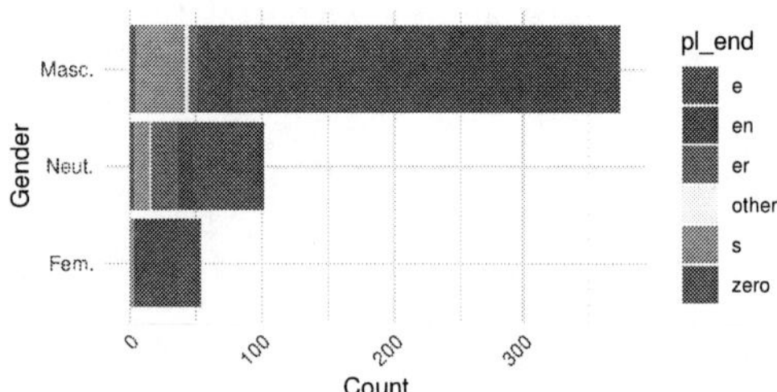

Figure 3: Distribution of plural suffix by gender for consonant-final monosyllabic words in UniMorph

	Overall-TF	Gender-TF
Speakers	**.78** (.73, .82)	.70 (.64, .75)
ED	.47 (.33, .59)	**.71** (.61, .78)

Table 2: Correlations (Pearson's *r*, 95% CI in parens) between item-level production percentages for speakers and ED model with 1) overall type frequency (Overall-TF), 2) gender-conditioned type frequency (Gender-TF), *only* considering consonant-final monosyllabic nouns in UniMorph (shown in Figure 3).

5 Discussion

We hypothesized that adult speakers and neural encoder-decoder models would make similar use of grammatical gender when inflecting novel words in the plural, as gender is a salient and consistent cue to plural inflection class, especially in an experimental setup where semantic cues are absent. Contrary to expectations, our results indicate that both learners attend to grammatical gender, but to different degrees — the neural model is much *more* sensitive to grammatical gender than adult speakers, whose productions are closer to the overall type frequency of plural suffixes in German.

The neural model's use of grammatical gender is not surprising, as it aligns with earlier findings (c.f. Goebel and Indefrey, 2000); however, the speakers' *lack* of attention to gender is unexpected. In their large-scale production study with the same noun stimuli, Zaretsky and Lange (2016) found reliable effects of grammatical gender: their participants used -(e)n for 33% of feminine nouns, versus 19% of non-feminine nouns (compare to our study: 33% vs. 26%). -e also appeared more with nonfeminine nouns (49% vs. 41%), although the effect was not statistically significant. Nonetheless, they note that -e was most frequently produced for feminine nouns as well as nonfeminine nouns, consistent with our results, and their data shows a similarly broad distribution over types. Despite other differences between our study design and theirs (e.g. online vs. in-person data collection, typed vs. written modality, German speakers from various backgrounds vs. one region), we consider our results fundamentally aligned: speakers show a slight but statistically reliable effect of gender on -(e)n and -e production, in both cases much less than the effect shown by the ED model.

One possibility is that the phonological forms of our noun stimuli provide their own statistical conditioning, to a stronger degree than anticipated. This

is illustrated in Figure 3, which plots the distribution of nouns in UniMorph sharing two key properties with our stimuli: they are monosyllabic and end in a consonant. On the one hand, nouns with this type of form clearly also show gender conditioning, with -(e)n much more prevalent among feminine nouns. On the other hand, nouns with this general form are predominantly masculine gender, and the numerical prevalence of nonfeminine forms may diminish speakers' sensitivity to a rare feminine gender cue, such as they encounter in our experiment. Under this account, adult speakers condition their plural productions upon phonological form to a greater extent than grammatical gender. The results in Table 2 further support this interpretation. Looking only at the consonant-final monosyllabic words plotted in Figure 3, ED model productions show a higher correlation to the gender-conditioned distribution over plural suffixes, while the highest correlation generally (.78) appears between speakers productions and the overall distribution of plural classes for these phonologically similar words. The potential shortcoming of the ED as a cognitive model, then, is that it assigns too much weight to the cue of grammatical gender, even though it is statistically reasonable to do so.

In conclusion, our comparison of neural encoder-decoder models and adult German speakers found a significant difference in their use of grammatical gender as a cue to plural inflection. Although this cue is highly informative, speakers — unlike neural models — appear relatively insensitive to gender in our task. This finding suggests that speakers may attend more readily to other cues such as phonology, and therefore match productions to a different distribution which shows less gender conditioning.

Acknowledgments

This work was supported in part by the EPSRC Centre for Doctoral Training in Data Science, funded by the UK Engineering and Physical Sciences Research Council (grant EP/L016427/1) and the University of Edinburgh, and a James S McDonnell Foundation Scholar Award (#220020374) to the third author.

References

Douglas Bates, Martin Mächler, Ben Bolker, and Steve Walker. 2015. Fitting Linear Mixed-Effects Models Using lme4. *Journal of Statistical Software*, 67(1):1–48.

Jean Berko. 1958. The Child's Learning of English Morphology. *WORD*, 14(2-3):150–177.

Maria Corkery, Yevgen Matusevych, and Sharon Goldwater. 2019. Are we there yet? Encoder-decoder neural networks as cognitive models of English past tense inflection. In *Proceedings of the 57th Conference of the Association for Computational Linguistics*, pages 3868–3877, Florence, Italy. Association for Computational Linguistics.

Jennifer Culbertson, Annie Gagliardi, and Kenny Smith. 2017. Competition between phonological and semantic cues in noun class learning. *Journal of Memory and Language*, 92:343–358.

Lenore Frigo and Janet L. McDonald. 1998. Properties of Phonological Markers That Affect the Acquisition of Gender-Like Subclasses. *Journal of Memory and Language*, 39(2):218–245.

Rainer Goebel and Peter Indefrey. 2000. A recurrent network with short-term memory capacity learning the German-s plural. *Models of language acquisition: Inductive and deductive approaches*, pages 177–200.

Peter Indefrey. 1999. Some problems with the lexical status of nondefault inflection. *Behavioral and Brain Sciences*, 22(6):1025–1025.

Katharina Kann and Hinrich Schütze. 2016. Single-Model Encoder-Decoder with Explicit Morphological Representation for Reinflection. In *Proceedings of the 54th Annual Meeting of the Association for Computational Linguistics (Volume 2: Short Papers)*, pages 555–560, Berlin, Germany. Association for Computational Linguistics.

David L King, Andrea D Sims, and Micha Elsner. 2020. Interpreting Sequence-to-Sequence Models for Russian Inflectional Morphology. In *Proceedings of the Society for Computation in Linguistics*, volume 3.

Christo Kirov and Ryan Cotterell. 2018. Recurrent Neural Networks in Linguistic Theory: Revisiting Pinker and Prince (1988) and the Past Tense Debate. *Transactions of the Association for Computational Linguistics*, 6:651–665.

Christo Kirov, John Sylak-Glassman, Roger Que, and David Yarowsky. 2016. Very-large Scale Parsing and Normalization of Wiktionary Morphological Paradigms. In *Proceedings of the Tenth International Conference on Language Resources and Evaluation (LREC 2016)*, pages 3121–3126, Portorož, Slovenia. European Language Resources Association (ELRA).

Klaus-Michael Köpcke. 1988. Schemas in German plural formation. *Lingua*, 74(4):303–335.

Sabine Laaha, Dorit Ravid, Katharina Korecky-Kröll, Gregor Laaha, and Wolfgang U. Dressler. 2006. Early noun plurals in German: regularity, productivity or default? *Journal of Child Language*, 33(2):271–302.

Brian MacWhinney. 1978. The Acquisition of Morphophonology. *Monographs of the Society for Research in Child Development*, 43(1/2):1.

Gary F Marcus, Ursula Brinkmann, Harald Clahsen, Richard Wiese, and Steven Pinker. 1995. German inflection: The exception that proves the rule. *Cognitive psychology*, 29(3):189–256.

Kate McCurdy, Sharon Goldwater, and Adam Lopez. 2020. Inflecting When There's No Majority: Limitations of Encoder-Decoder Neural Networks as Cognitive Models for German Plurals. In *Proceedings of the 58th Annual Meeting of the Association for Computational Linguistics*, pages 1745–1756, Online. Association for Computational Linguistics.

Elissa L. Newport. 2016. Statistical language learning: computational, maturational, and linguistic constraints. *Language and Cognition*, 8(3):447–461.

R Core Team. 2019. *R: A Language and Environment for Statistical Computing*. R Foundation for Statistical Computing, Vienna, Austria.

Ilya Sutskever, Oriol Vinyals, and Quoc V Le. 2014. Sequence to Sequence Learning with Neural Networks. In *Advances in Neural Information Processing Systems*, pages 3104–3112.

Adina Williams, Tiago Pimentel, Hagen Blix, Arya D. McCarthy, Eleanor Chodroff, and Ryan Cotterell. 2020. Predicting Declension Class from Form and Meaning. In *Proceedings of the 58th Annual Meeting of the Association for Computational Linguistics*, pages 6682–6695, Online. Association for Computational Linguistics.

Charles D. Yang. 2016. *The price of linguistic productivity : how children learn to break the rules of language*. The MIT Press, Cambridge, Massachusetts.

Eugen Zaretsky and Benjamin P Lange. 2016. No matter how hard we try: Still no default plural marker in nonce nouns in Modern High German. In *A blend of MaLT: selected contributions from the Methods and Linguistic Theories Symposium 2015*, number Band 15 in Bamberger Beiträge zur Linguistik, pages 153–178. University of Bamberg Press, Bamberg.

Eugen Zaretsky, Benjamin P. Lange, Harald A. Euler, and Katrin Neumann. 2013. Acquisition of German pluralization rules in monolingual and multilingual children. *Studies in Second Language Learning and Teaching*, 3(4):551.

Suffix	Fixed effect	Est. β	Std. Err.	z value	$Pr(> |z|)$
-(e)n	(Intercept)	-1.51086	0.24064	-6.278	3.42e-10 ***
	gender.masc	-1.01487	0.08248	-12.304	< 2e-16 ***
	gender.neut	-0.39048	0.06956	-5.613	1.99e-08 ***
	source.ED	-0.09325	0.15534	-0.600	0.548
	gender.m:src.ED	-0.81875	0.08209	-9.974	< 2e-16 ***
	gender.n:src.ED	-0.27620	0.06944	-3.978	6.96e-05 ***
-e	(Intercept)	0.37876	0.18847	2.010	0.044473 *
	gender.masc	0.31680	0.05581	5.676	1.38e-08 ***
	gender.neut	0.58894	0.05727	10.283	< 2e-16 ***
	source.ED	0.43671	0.13094	3.335	0.000852 ***
	gender.m:src.ED	0.42172	0.05586	7.549	4.38e-14 ***
	gender.n:src.ED	0.41830	0.05713	7.322	2.44e-13 ***

Table 3: Summary of fixed effects from logistic regression analysis

Rhymes	Non-Rhymes
Bral	Bnaupf
Kach	Bneik
Klot	Bnöhk
Mur	Fnahf
Nuhl	Fneik
Pind	Fnöhk
Pisch	Plaupf
Pund	Pleik
Raun	Pläk
Spand	Pnähf
Spert	Pröng
Vag	Snauk

Table 4: Experimental stimuli (Marcus et al., 1995)

A Stimuli

Table 4 shows the 24 noun stimuli used in our experiment. In their original study, Marcus et al. distinguished between Rhymes, which rhyme with existing German words, and Non-Rhymes, which don't. As this distinction is not relevant to our study, we omit it from our analysis.

B Statistical analysis

Here we report the results of our statistical model of the production of -e and -(e)n. We fit two separate mixed-effect binomial logistic models using the lme4 package (Bates et al., 2015) in R (R Core Team, 2019). Item (i.e. stimulus word) and subject (participant for human study, random seed for ED model) were included as random effects. Both models were fit using a stepwise procedure. We started with a baseline model of intercept plus random effects and incrementally added the following fixed effects (with sum-coded contrasts): grammatical gender (masculine coded as 1, neuter as 2, feminine not contrasted), data source (ED model coded as 1, speakers not contrasted), gender by source interaction. Each additional fixed effect produced a significantly improved fit as measured by a chi-squared test.

The final model for both -e and -(e)n production includes all fixed and random effects described above. For both plural suffixes, model results indicate a significant main effect of gender from both speakers and the ED model, and a significant interaction with data source, corresponding to a stronger effect of gender from ED model productions. For -e productions, there is also a main effect of data source: the ED model reliably produces -e more than speakers do overall. The -(e)n model shows no significant main effect for source. When model predictions are transformed to responses and fit to the original data, the binomial model of -e production achieves an overall predictive accuracy of 75% (precision 0.77, recall 0.79, F1 0.78), while the -(e)n model has 82% predictive accuracy (precision 0.71, recall 0.59, F1 0.65).

Sanity checks As human speakers show high inter-participant variability on this task (Fig. 4), we performed additional separate analysis on the speaker data.[8] We fit the same model as previously described, with the exception that the data source factor was omitted, as all data came from speakers. We also fit models using Masculine and Neuter as the reference gender in the sum contrast coding scheme, to see whether they yielded different results from the original model's Feminine reference level.

---

[8]We thank an anonymous reviewer for highlighting this issue and suggesting these validity checks.

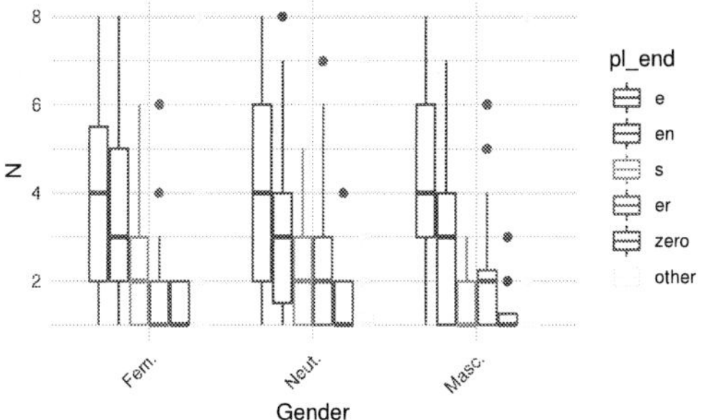

Figure 4: Individual speaker variation in plural suffix production by gender. Each speaker saw 8 words from each gender, shown on the y-axis. For each gender and plural suffix, the boxes indicate the median and interquartile range of individual speaker productions for that combination. For all gender categories, the median number of -e productions is 4, while the median number of -(e)n productions is 3.

Suffix	Effect	Fem.	Neut.
-(e)n	gdr.fem	.	.31 (.08) ***
	gdr.neut	-.19 (.08) *	.
	gdr.masc	-.12 (.08)	-.12 (.08)
-e	gdr.fem	.	-.07 (.07)
	gdr.neut	-.1 (.07)	.
	gdr.masc	.17 (.07) *	.17 (.07) *

Table 5: Speaker data only: statistical effect of different gender reference levels in contrast coding. Header shows reference level, cells show estimated coefficient (standard error in parentheses). Estimates for Masculine reference level are identical to rows already shown (e.g. suffix -(e)n: $-.19$ for gdr.neut, .31 for gdr.fem). Stars indicate significance level: $* \leq 0.05$, $** \leq 0.01$, $*** \leq 0.001$.

The speaker-only model shows a reduced but consistent effect of gender (Tab. 5). Speakers reliably produce -(e)n more for feminine nouns, and less for neuter nouns, relative to the grand mean. Speakers also reliably produce -e more for masculine nouns. These difference are statistically significant even though, for all three genders, speakers produce -e more than -(e)n (Fig. 4).

Learning Pronoun Case from Distributional Cues:
Flexible Frames for Case Acquisition

Xiaomeng Ma[1], Martin Chodorow[1,2], Virginia Valian[1,2]
[1]The Graduate Center and [2]Hunter College, CUNY
xma3@gradcenter.cuny.edu, mchodorow@hunter.cuny.edu, vvalian@gc.cuny.com

Abstract

Case is an abstract grammatical feature that indicates argument relationship in a sentence. In English, cases are expressed on pronouns, as nominative case (e.g. *I*, *he*), accusative case(e.g. *me*, *him*) and genitive case (e.g. *my*, *his*). Children correctly use cased pronouns at a very young age. How do they acquire abstract case in the first place when different cases are not associated with different meanings? This paper proposes that the distributional patterns in parents' input could be used to distinguish grammatical cases in English.

1 Introduction

Case is a special grammatical property of nouns, pronouns, adjectives, participles or numerals whose value reflects the grammatical function performed by that word in a phrase, clause or sentence. In some languages, all of the word categories mentioned above take different inflected forms depending on their case. English, however, has largely lost its inflected cases and only expresses three cases on personal pronouns: nominative case (e.g. *I, he, she*), accusative case (e.g. *me, him*) and genitive case (e.g. *my, his, her*). These cases are used to mark different relationships between arguments and are commonly referred to as abstract case. For example, nominative pronouns are used as the subject of the sentence; accusative pronouns are used as the objects; and genitive pronouns are used as determiners. Case is formally assigned by the +FI-NITE feature in the syntactic projection.

English-speaking children are able to use cased pronouns correctly at a very early age. However, between ages 2-4, they reportedly make pronoun case errors such as 'where does *him* go'[1], 'all

of *they* going go in here'[2] and 'what *my* doing'[3]. These errors might provide insights into how children acquire grammatical case. For over 40 years, researchers have proposed different explanations of abstract case acquisition based on such errors (e.g. Huxley, 1970; Budwig, 1989; Rispoli, 2005; Fitzgerald et al., 2017). The syntactic explanation argues that children's knowledge of grammatical case is the result of syntactic maturation of the tense and agreement system (Vainikka, 1993; Wexler, 1994; Schütze and Wexler, 1996). The morphosyntactic theory proposes that children form a paradigm for each pronoun, including features like case, person, gender and number and retrieve different forms for different contexts (Rispoli, 1994, 1998).

In addition, parents' input has been implicated to play an important role in case acquisition. Previous studies have argued that some of the children's pronoun case errors could be explained by the ambiguous uses of pronouns in parents' input. For example, Pelham (2011) argued that English-speaking children made more pronoun case errors than German-speaking children because there are more case-ambiguous pronouns (e.g. *you* and *it*) in English. Tomasello (2000) suggested that children could be confused by phrases such as 'Let *me* do it', thus producing errors like '*me* do it'.

Are children able to learn pronoun case in the face of ambiguity? We investigated whether parents' input is informative enough for children to learn pronominal case. In English, nominative, accusative, and genitive case have different distributional patterns. For example, nominative pronouns are more likely to occur before a verb (e.g. '*I* see'), whereas accusative or genitive pronouns

---

[1]Utterance from Becky at 2;6 in the Manchester corpus (Theakston et al., 2001), Manchester/Becky/020619.cha

[2]Utterance from Nina at 2;11 in the Suppes corpus (Suppes, 1974), Suppes/021021.cha

[3]Utterance from Eve at 2;1 in the Brown corpus (Brown, 1973), Brown/Eve/020100b.cha

Proceedings of the Workshop on Cognitive Modeling and Computational Linguistics, pages 66–74
Online Event, November 19, 2020. ©2020 Association for Computational Linguistics
https://doi.org/10.18653/v1/P17

rarely appear before a verb (e.g. '*me/my* see'). However, cases do not have exclusive distributional patterns. Some patterns are shared by more than one case: an accusative pronoun case precede a verb in phrases like 'let *him* go' or 'help *me* see.' (Tomasello, 2000). Therefore, we asked if patterns of word co-occurrence could be used to differentiate pronoun cases. In the section 2, we review prior approaches using co-occurrence patterns for word categorization. In section 3, we introduce our methods and models. In section 4, we explain the setup and results of three analyses. Section 5 summarizes our contributions.

2   Related Work

Distributional information can be effective in grammatical categorization tasks. Redington et al. (1998) demonstrated that the context of a target word, including the previous words and following words, can be used to cluster the target word into different grammatical categories. Their model achieved high accuracy in categorization in general; however, for words that appear in less frequent contexts, accuracy suffered. Mintz (2003) proposed that frequent local trigram frames consisting of one word before the target word and one word following it (an aXb frame, where X is the target word) contain enough information for grammatical categorization. For example, in the frame 'to X to', X is likely to be a verb, e.g. 'to go to'. Mintz examined the 45 most frequent aXb frames in parents' input and showed that the accuracy for X's grammatical categorization was over 0.90. However, only a small portion of words appear in the frequent aXb frames. In order to categorize more words, Clair et al. (2010) separated the aXb frame into two bigram frames: aX + Xb. They suggested that instead of learning the co-occurring frame 'a_b' as a whole unit, it is more efficient to treat it as two flexible bigrams 'a_' and '_b' which are more useful in learning. They trained feedforward neural networks on 100,000 samples of the aXb frame and the aX + Xb frame had better categorization accuracy (0.73) than the aXb frame (0.53).

Grammatical cases are similar to grammatical categories in that both reflect certain syntactic features of the word. In this paper, we trained models to predict the pronoun case of X using aXb and aX + Xb frames. The purpose of the study is not to provide a model to explain children's grammatical case acquisition, but to examine if the distributional

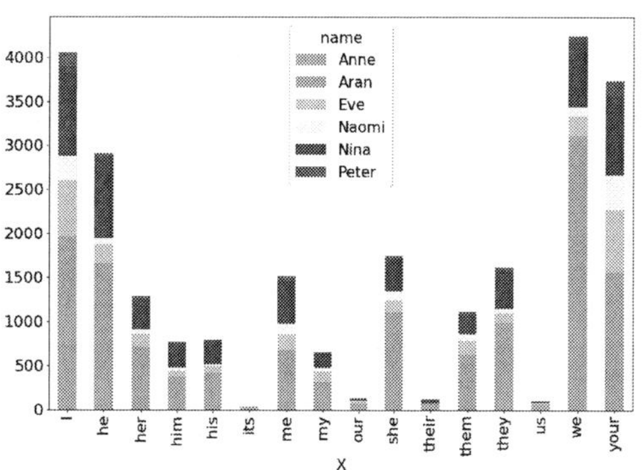

Figure 1: Pronoun tokens by the parents of six children

patterns in parents' input are informative enough to distinguish pronoun cases. The results do not indicate whether children acquire pronoun case from parents' input but suggest a possible source from which children could learn pronoun case.

3   Methods

3.1   Corpus Summary

Following Mintz (2003) and Clair et al. (2010), we used the same six corpora of child-directed speech from CHILDES (MacWhinney, 2014): Anne and Aran (Theakston et al., 2001), Eve (Brown, 1973), Naomi (Sachs, 1983), Nina (Suppes, 1974), Peter (Bloom et al., 1974). We analyzed the utterances in the files where the child is younger than 2;6 years old. The pronouns were extracted with the part-of-speech tags assigned by the MOR parser (MacWhinney, 2012) in CHILDES: pro:sub for nominative pronouns, pro:obj for accusative pronouns and det:poss for genitive pronouns. Case-ambiguous pronouns 'you' and 'it' were excluded from the study since they were tagged as pro:per in all argument positions. The pronoun 'her' was included since it was tagged as pro:obj for its accusative use and det:poss for its genitive use. Each pronoun was extracted with its aXb context. Table 1 summarizes the number of tokens of all pronouns and each case, and the number of types for aX, Xb and aXb. Figure 1 shows the token frequencies of the pronouns produced by the children's parents.

3.2   Model Architecture

We used supervised learning with a feedforward connectionist model to compare the accuracy of the aXb model and the aX + Xb model. For the aXb

	Nominative	Accusative	Genitive	Pronoun Tokens	aX types	Xb types	aXb types
Aran	4518	1014	1454	6986	445	927	2489
Anne	4343	1080	1392	6815	428	707	2308
Eve	1292	479	1029	2800	278	500	1364
Naomi	599	249	503	1352	224	364	806
Nina	3490	1195	1571	6256	400	747	2376
Peter	339	135	207	681	187	250	475
Total	14581	4152	6156	24889	898	1672	7355

Table 1: Token counts of three pronoun cases and type counts of three context frames

model, the input consisted of one one-hot vector, representing 'a_b'. For the aX + Xb model, the input consisted of two one-hot vectors, representing 'a_' and '_b' respectively. The two models are shown in Figure 2 and Figure 3, with 'let me do' as an example. For the aXb model, the input unit represents 'let_do'. For the aX + Xb model, one input represents 'let_' and the other input represents '_do'. The connectionist model used the following parameters: (1) number of hidden units was set to 200 and initialized randomly for each model; (2) the non-linearity was relu.

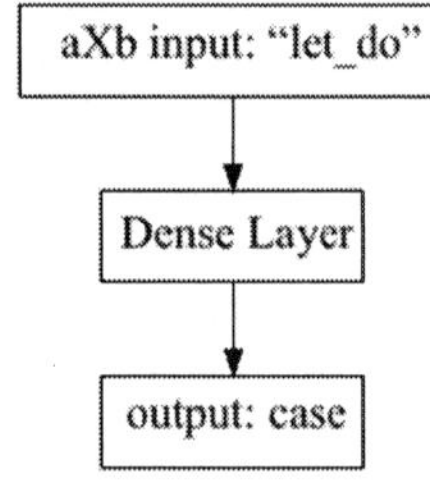

Figure 2: The architecture of aXb model

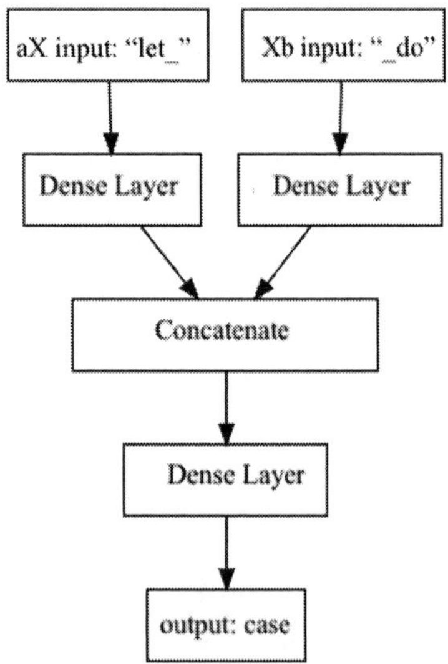

Figure 3: The architecture of aX + Xb model

3.3 Evaluation

We use the classification accuracy for each case to compare the aXb model and aX + Xb models. In addition, following Clair et al. (2010) we also report the asymmetric lambda value Goodman and Kruskal (1979) to evaluate the association among the classification of grammatical cases. Lambda is defined as the proportional reduction in prediction error. It provides insight into the extent to which the model's prediction is based on the actual category. Lambda is in the range of [0,1], where 0 indicates there is no association between predicted and actual categories, and 1 indicates a perfect association. For example, if the model categorizes all frames as nominative cases simply because that is the most frequent case, then the accuracy will be 0.586 (14581/24889), but the lambda will be 0.

3.4 Training and Testing

We measured and compared the classification accuracy of models by applying 10-fold cross validation on the union of the six children's corpora. The aXb model and aX + Xb model were trained using the same 10-fold cross-validation split. All the frames were used for both training and testing.

We used the Adam optimization algorithm to minimize the mean squared error (MSE) loss function over the training data. We trained the model on a maximum of 100 epochs with a batch size of 32. Early stopping methods were applied to stop the training when the accuracy did not change in 10 consecutive training rounds.

4 Experiments

4.1 Experiment 1: Models aXb vs aX + Xb in Categorizing Grammatical Cases

Method. All models were trained and evaluated following the steps in Section 3. Following (Clair et al., 2010), we split the training of each model into a token-training phase and a type-training phase. In the token-training phase, we trained the models on all 24889 pronoun patterns. In the type-training phase, we trained the models only on 7355 tokens of unique aXb types.

Results of two training phases Tables 2 and 3 show the overall classification accuracies and lambda scores of aXb and aX + Xb on each child's corpus. Both models achieved very high accuracy with 24889 tokens. In addition, the lambda scores showed that almost perfect associations, suggesting that the aXb and aX + Xb models are very effective in predicting the correct grammatical case. Figures 4 and 5 show the heatmaps of the classification results. All three cases are classified with high accuracy. The heatmaps also indicate that the two models make different classification errors. For example, for genitive case, the aX + Xb model is more likely to miscategorize it as an accusative case whereas the aXb model is more likely to label it as a nominative case.

	aX + Xb		aXb	
	Accuracy	λ	**Accuracy**	λ
Aran	0.984	0.956	0.962	0.894
Anne	0.984	0.957	0.962	0.897
Eve	0.979	0.961	0.960	0.928
Naomi	0.983	0.969	0.951	0.914
Nina	0.987	0.970	0.951	0.911
Peter	0.982	0.965	0.954	0.913
Total	**0.984**	**0.962**	**0.960**	**0.907**

Table 2: Results of training on 24889 total tokens

	aX + Xb		aXb	
	Accuracy	λ	**Accuracy**	λ
Aran	0.968	0.940	0.849	0.631
Anne	0.963	0.936	0.841	0.639
Eve	0.968	0.931	0.872	0.648
Naomi	0.953	0.902	0.878	0.708
Nina	0.974	0.952	0.834	0.600
Peter	0.963	0.927	0.827	0.619
Total	**0.967**	**0.939**	**0.847**	**0.631**

Table 3: Results of Training on 7355 tokens of unique types

When the sample size drops to 7355 tokens, the accuracies and the lambda scores also change for both models. The performance of aX + Xb is not heavily affected by a smaller sample size: the accuracy changes from 0.984 to 0.967 and the lambda score changes from 0.962 to 0.939. In contrast,

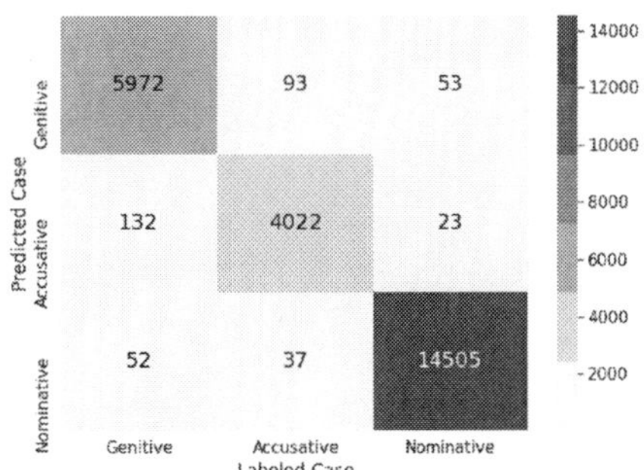

Figure 4: Heatmap of each case's classification in aX + Xb model of 24889 total tokens

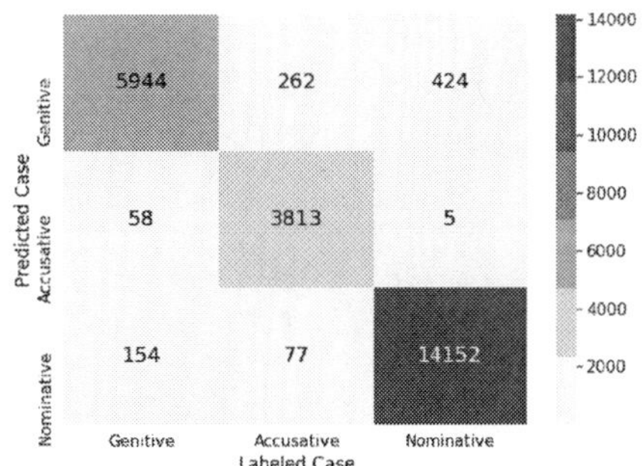

Figure 5: Heatmap of each case's classification in aXb model of 24889 total tokens

the aXb model shows a large decline in the accuracy and the lambda score when the sample size drops: the accuracy falls to 0.847 and the lambda score drops to 0.631. Thus, aX + Xb not only has higher accuracy, but also is less vulnerable to small sample size. Figures 6 and 7 are the classification heatmaps of each case. We also plotted the classification accuracies of each pronoun for each child's input, which can be found in Figures 11 - 14 in the Appendix.

4.2 Experiment 2: Predicting the Pronoun Using aX + Xb Model with Person, Gender, Number Information

Method. Since the aX + Xb model achieved high accuracy in grammatical case classification, we asked if the pronoun can be effectively predicted when person, gender and number information are given in training. In the second experiment, we coded the person, gender, and number information for each pronoun (e.g. 'he' would be coded as third-person, masculine and singular) and added it as an additional input to the aX + Xb model. We

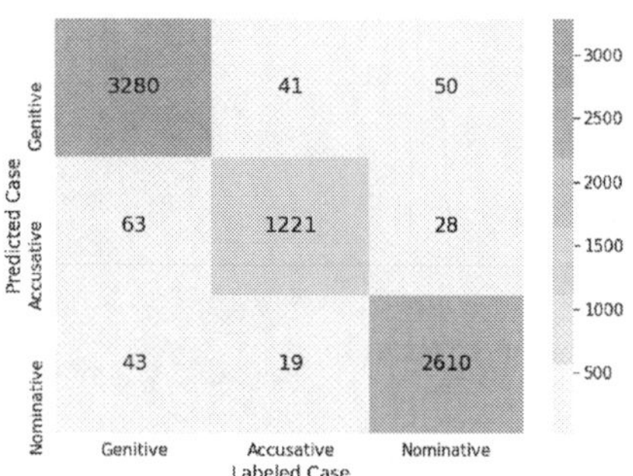

Figure 6: Heatmap of each case's classification in `aX + Xb` model of 7355 tokens of unique types

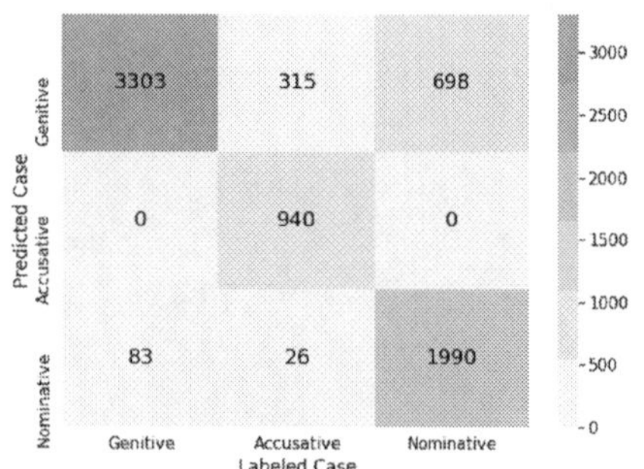

Figure 7: Heatmap of each case's classification in `aXb` model of 7355 tokens of unique types

trained the model on the same 24889 total tokens and 7355 tokens of unique types as in Experiment 1, and used the same 10-fold cross-validation splits.

Results. Table 4 shows the results. With gender, person and number as additional input, the `aX + Xb` model can predict the pronoun at an accuracy of 0.994 with 24889 total tokens and 0.982 with 7355 tokens of unique types. In addition, the lambda scores indicate an almost perfect association. Given additional information on person, gender, and number, the `aX + Xb` model is extremely effective in predicting the pronoun.

Figures 8 and 9 show the classification results for each pronoun. The classification errors on each pronoun are usually case errors (e.g. 'I' mislabeled as 'me' or 'my'). There are few errors on the gender (e.g. 'he' mislabeled as 'she') and almost no errors on number and person. Each child's pronoun accuracy in shown in Figures 15 and 16 in the Appendix.

	24889 tokens		7355 types	
	Accuracy	λ	**Accuracy**	λ
Aran	0.994	0.992	0.980	0.971
Anne	0.994	0.992	0.980	0.976
Eve	0.993	0.990	0.983	0.972
Naomi	0.993	0.995	0.980	0.967
Nina	0.996	0.994	0.987	0.982
Peter	1.000	1.000	0.983	0.975
Total	**0.994**	**0.993**	**0.982**	**0.975**

Table 4: Results of `aX + Xb` model Predicting Pronoun on 24889 and 7355 tokens with gender, number, person information

4.3 Experiment 3: Corpus Analysis of Children's Pronoun Case Error Patterns

Experiments 1 and 2 have show that distributional patterns are extremely effective in pronoun case categorization, suggesting that parents' input is informative for pronoun case learning. In experiment 3, we examine how well children learn pronouns. We conducted a corpus analysis of all six children's utterances and calculated their pronoun case errors.

Methods. We searched the pronoun case errors in each child's utterances in all available files (including those with an age older than 2;6) in the corpora. To identify pronoun case errors, the part-of-speech tags in CHILDES were used. For English data, the automated annotation system has been reported to have high-level accuracy: the MOR program reaches 97% accuracy in word categorization, and the GRASP program has 95.8% accuracy in determining the subject in the sentence and 94.1% accuracy in determining the object in the sentence (MacWhinney, 2012; Sagae et al., 2010). After the errors were first located using the MOR program and GRASP programs, two annotators independently hand-checked the errors.

Results. Table 5 shows the accuracy for each child's pronoun case use. Most children have very high accuracy in their pronoun case uses, except for Nina, whose accuracy is 0.926. The overall pronoun case accuracy for all 6 children is 0.97, which is similar to the results of the `aX + Xb` model (0.967 for unique types and 0.984 for total tokens).

Figure 10 shows children's errors on pronoun cases. Children's errors are different from the classification models' errors. Children never mistreated a genitive pronoun or a nominative pronoun as an accusative pronoun.

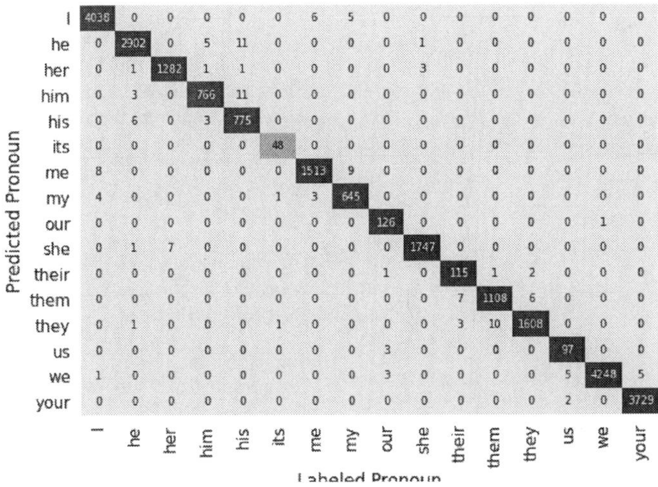

Figure 8: Heatmap of pronoun classification results on 24889 total tokens

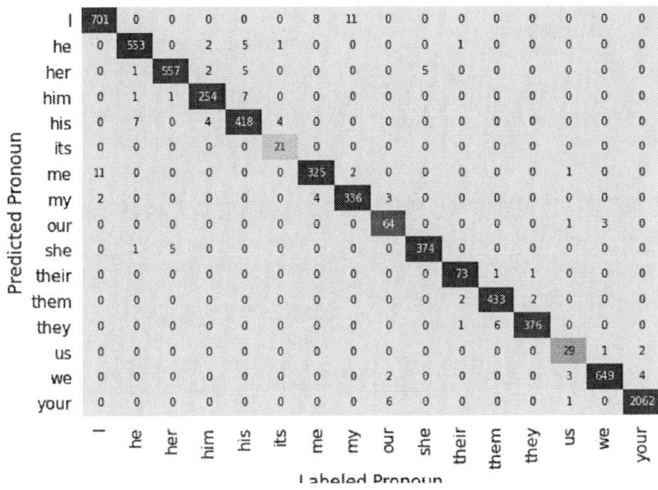

Figure 9: Heatmap of pronoun classification results on 7355 tokens of unique types

5   Discussion and Conclusion

In this work, we proposed that distribution patterns could be used to distinguish pronoun cases. We trained models on the fixed trigram frame aXb and flexible frame aX + Xb with a large sample size and a smaller one. The results showed that the distributional patterns are extremely effective in categorizing grammatical case of pronouns. Based on the high accuracy results with case categorization, we further explored pronoun categorization with person, gender, and number information as additional input. With large sample size, our model achieved almost perfect pronoun categorization ac-

curacy. We then conducted a corpus analysis to examine children's pronoun case acquisition. Most of the children have a similar accuracy rate as our training model.

Our experiments showed that distributional patterns in parents' input are very useful in categorizing grammatical cases. Our model showed a similar accuracy rate as children's real-life pronoun case acquisition. However, the similar accuracy rate does not demonstrate that children actually utilize distributional patterns in learning and the differences between the errors made by training models and by children suggest children may be

71

	Errors	Total Pronouns	Accuracy
Anne	57	5009	0.989
Aran	25	8450	0.997
Peter	115	4077	0.971
Eve	49	2685	0.982
Naomi	64	3249	0.980
Nina	633	8609	0.926
Total	**943**	**32079**	**0.970**

Table 5: Results of each child's pronoun case errors and accuracy

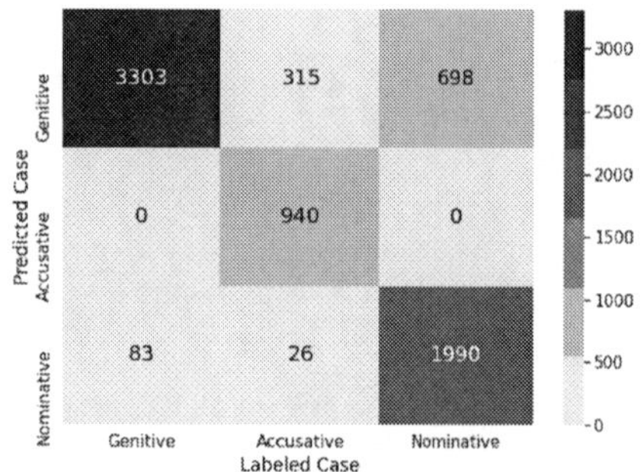

Figure 10: Heatmap of pronoun case uses by children

using a different procedure or an additional procedure. Further investigations of the classification errors and children's pronoun case errors will be informative for understanding the process of case categorization.

References

Lois Bloom, Lois Hood, and Patsy Lightbown. 1974. Imitation in language development: If, when, and why. *Cognitive psychology*, 6(3):380–420.

Roger Brown. 1973. *A first language: The early stages.* Harvard U. Press.

Nancy Budwig. 1989. The linguistic marking of agentivity and control in child language. *Journal of Child Language*, 16(2):263–284.

Michelle C St Clair, Padraic Monaghan, and Morten H Christiansen. 2010. Learning grammatical categories from distributional cues: Flexible frames for language acquisition. *Cognition*, 116(3):341–360.

Colleen E Fitzgerald, Matthew Rispoli, and Pamela A Hadley. 2017. Case marking uniformity in developmental pronoun errors. *First Language*, 37(4):391–409.

Leo A Goodman and William H Kruskal. 1979. Measures of association for cross classifications. In *Measures of association for cross classifications*, pages 2–34. Springer.

Renira Huxley. 1970. The development of the correct use of subject personal pronouns in two children. In Flores D'arcais, G.B., and Levelt, W. J. M. (eds.). *Advances in Psycholinguistics*, pages 141–165.

Brian MacWhinney. 2012. Morphosyntactic analysis of the childes and talkbank corpora. In *LREC*, pages 2375–2380.

Brian MacWhinney. 2014. *The CHILDES project: Tools for analyzing talk, Volume II: The database.* Psychology Press.

Toben H Mintz. 2003. Frequent frames as a cue for grammatical categories in child directed speech. *Cognition*, 90(1):91–117.

Sabra D Pelham. 2011. The input ambiguity hypothesis and case blindness: an account of cross-linguistic and intra-linguistic differences in case errors. *Journal of Child Language*, 38(2):235–272.

Martin Redington, Nick Chater, and Steven Finch. 1998. Distributional information: A powerful cue for acquiring syntactic categories. *Cognitive Science*, 22(4):425–469.

Matthew Rispoli. 1994. Pronoun case overextensions and paradigm building. *Journal of Child Language*, 21(1):157–172.

Matthew Rispoli. 1998. Me or my: Two different patterns of pronoun case errors. *Journal of Speech, Language, and Hearing Research*, 41(2):385–393.

Matthew Rispoli. 2005. When children reach beyond their grasp: Why some children make pronoun case errors and others don't. *Journal of Child Language*, 32(1):93–116.

Jacqueline Sachs. 1983. Talking about the there and then: The emergence of displaced reference in parent-child discourse. *Children's Language*, 4:1–28.

Kenji Sagae, Eric Davis, Alon Lavie, Brian MacWhinney, and Shuly Wintner. 2010. Morphosyntactic annotation of childes transcripts. *Journal of Child Language*, 37(3):705–729.

Carson Schütze and Kenneth Wexler. 1996. Subject case licensing and English root infinitives. In *Proceedings of the 20th annual Boston University conference on language development*, volume 2, pages 670–681. Cascadilla Press Somerville, MA.

Patrick Suppes. 1974. The semantics of children's language. *American Psychologist*, 29(2):103.

Anna L Theakston, Elena VM Lieven, Julian M Pine, and Caroline F Rowland. 2001. The role of performance limitations in the acquisition of verb-argument structure: An alternative account. *Journal of Child Language*, 28(1):127–152.

Michael Tomasello. 2000. Do young children have adult syntactic competence? *Cognition*, 74(3):209–253.

Anne Vainikka. 1993. Case in the development of english syntax. *Language Acquisition*, 3(3):257–325.

Ken Wexler. 1994. 14 optional infinitives, head movement and the economy of derivations1. *Verb Movement*, page 305.

A Appendix

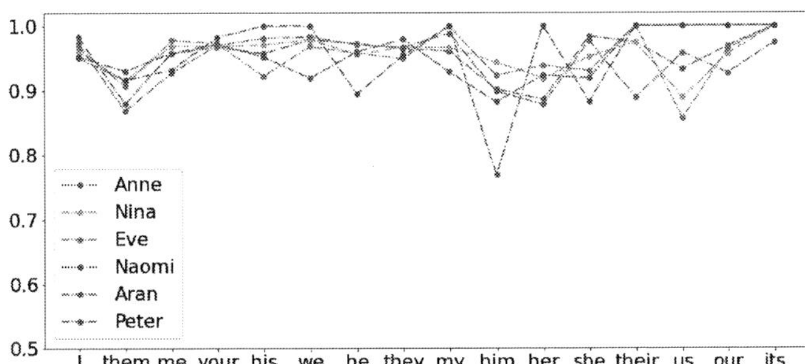

Figure 11: aXb model accuracy with 24889 total tokens

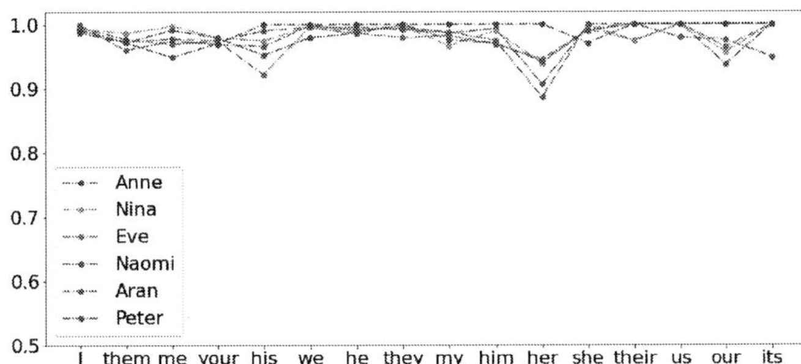

Figure 12: aX+Xb model accuracy with 24889 total tokens

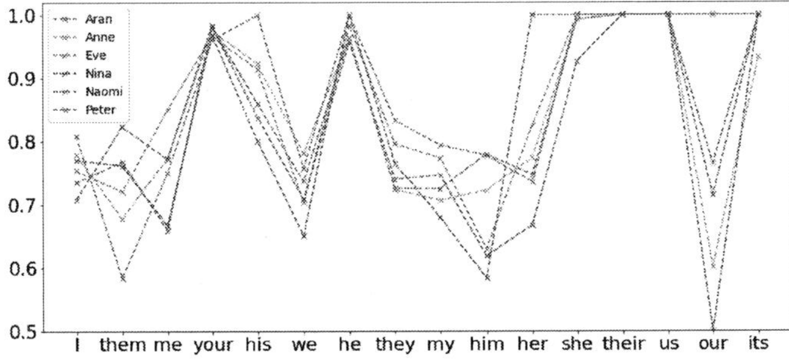

Figure 13: aXb model accuracy with 7355 tokens of unique types

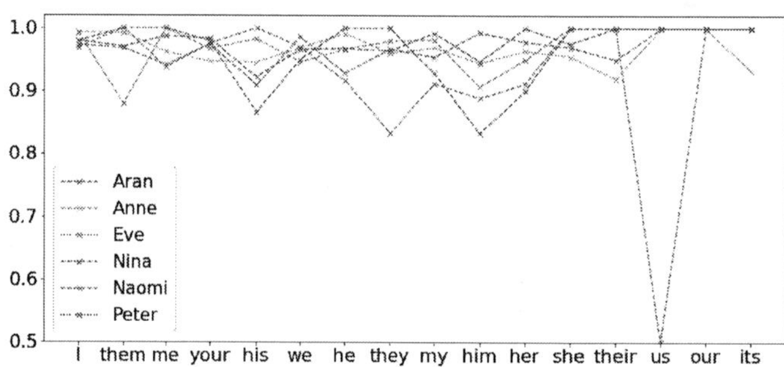

Figure 14: aX + Xb model accuracy for each pronoun with 7355 tokens of unique types

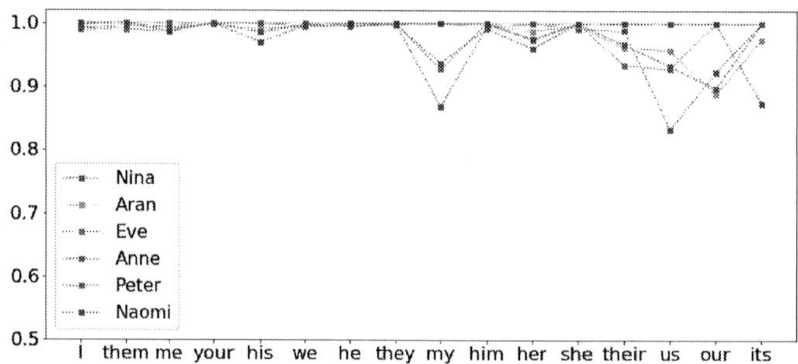

Figure 15: Accuracies of aX + Xb model with person, gender, number information for each pronoun with 24889 total tokens

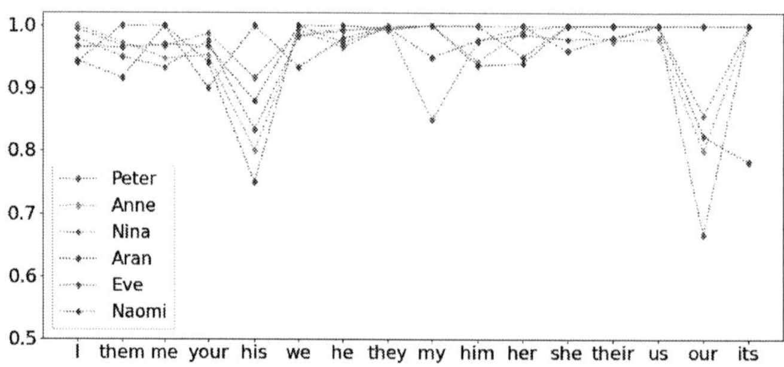

Figure 16: Accuracies of aX + Xb model with person, gender, number information for each pronoun with 7355 tokens of unique types

Probabilistic Predictions of People Perusing: Evaluating Metrics of Language Model Performance for Psycholinguistic Modeling

Yiding Hao, Simon Mendelsohn, Rachel Sterneck,
Randi Martinez, and **Robert Frank**
Yale University, New Haven, CT, USA
`firstname.lastname@yale.edu`

Abstract

By positing a relationship between naturalistic reading times and information-theoretic surprisal, surprisal theory (Hale, 2001; Levy, 2008) provides a natural interface between language models and psycholinguistic models. This paper re-evaluates a claim due to Goodkind and Bicknell (2018) that a language model's ability to model reading times is a linear function of its perplexity. By extending Goodkind and Bicknell's analysis to modern neural architectures, we show that the proposed relation does not always hold for Long Short-Term Memory networks, Transformers, and pre-trained models. We introduce an alternate measure of language modeling performance called *predictability norm correlation* based on Cloze probabilities measured from human subjects. Our new metric yields a more robust relationship between language model quality and psycholinguistic modeling performance that allows for comparison between models with different training configurations.

1   Introduction

Naturalistic reading times are known to be affected by incongruities between the current word and the context created by preceding words (Zola, 1981, 1984; Ehrlich and Rayner, 1981, *inter alia*). Words that are unexpected within their contexts are fixated for longer periods, while predictable words are fixated for a shorter amount of time or skipped altogether. This observation has been described formally by the suprisal theory of sentence processing (Hale, 2001; Levy, 2008), which posits that the difficulty of processing a particular word is directly proportional to its *surprisal*, defined as the negative logarithm of its probability given its preceding context.

By relating psychometric observations with information-theoretic concepts, surprisal theory provides a natural bridge between psycholinguistic modeling on the one hand and language modeling on the other. While modeling studies for reading times traditionally use surprisals obtained from probabilistic parsers (Hale, 2001; Demberg and Keller, 2008; Roark et al., 2009) or directly from probabilistic context-free grammars (Levy, 2008; Boston et al., 2008), surprisals from n-gram models (Mitchell et al., 2010; Smith and Levy, 2013) and simple recurrent network language models (Frank, 2009; Monsalve et al., 2012) have also been incorporated into reading-time studies. More recent work has sought to leverage the advances in language modeling made possible by neural NLP in order to determine whether modern techniques can yield more reliable estimates of surprisal for cognitive modeling. These studies have investigated the psycholinguistic capabilities of several neural architectures, including Long Short-Term Memory networks and Gated Recurrent Unit networks (Aurnhammer and Frank, 2019), Transformers (Merkx and Frank, 2020), and GPT-2 (Wilcox et al., 2020). In general, language models achieving a better *perplexity* have been found to yield better psycholinguistic models via the surprisal estimates they furnish, with Goodkind and Bicknell (2018) proposing a linear relationship between the two factors.

This paper revisits Goodkind and Bicknell's proposed linear relationship between perplexity and psycholinguistic modeling performance. We address two drawbacks of their analysis, which hinder its applicability to the state of the art in language modeling. Firstly, Goodkind and Bicknell only consider n-gram models and a small LSTM language model with 50 hidden units. These constitute a small and relatively weak collection of language models compared to the diverse array of techniques and vast computing resources that are available today. Secondly, the reliability of perplexity as a measure of language modeling performance is highly dependent on training configurations, such

75

Proceedings of the Workshop on Cognitive Modeling and Computational Linguistics, pages 75–86
Online Event, November 19, 2020. ©2020 Association for Computational Linguistics
https://doi.org/10.18653/v1/P17

that only perplexities for models with the same vocabulary are comparable (see Jurafsky and Martin, 2008, pp. 95–97). This is especially problematic given the rise of large-scale, general-purpose *pre-trained* language models, since vocabulary cannot be controlled for when comparing different pre-trained models.

To address these issues, we first expand Goodkind and Bicknell's empirical coverage by extending their analysis to Long Short-Term Memory networks (LSTMs, Hochreiter and Schmidhuber, 1997) and Transformers (Vaswani et al., 2017) of varying sizes and training corpora, along with four large pre-trained models. We then propose an alternate metric of language modeling performance based on word probabilities obtained from humans using a Cloze procedure (Taylor, 1953), which allows different pre-trained models to be compared with one another despite differences in vocabulary. In line with previous work, we find that the relationship between perplexity and psycholinguistic modeling performance is weaker for LSTMs and Transformers than for n-gram models, and not consistent across vocabularies. However, our Cloze-based metric yields a relationship which is robust to differences in model vocabulary and incorporates both our trained and our pre-trained models. Based on this, we argue that our Cloze-based metric is more suitable than perplexity for evaluating pre-trained models, and better reveals the relationship between language modeling performance and psycholinguistic modeling performance.

The structure of this paper is as follows. Section 2 describes our procedure for modeling reading times, and Section 3 describes our language models as well as the Cloze-based performance metric. Our results are presented in Section 4 and discussed in Section 5. Section 6 concludes.

2 Psycholinguistic Modeling

We follow the methodology of Goodkind and Bicknell (2018) for psycholinguistic modeling. We model reading times using generalized additive mixed-effect models (GAMMs), as implemented in the `mgcv` R package (Wood, 2004). Our GAMMs take several variables as input, optionally including language model surprisals. We fit a GAMM for each language model, along with a baseline model that does not include surprisal values. We measure the psycholinguistic modeling performance of each model by a score called *delta log likelihood*

(ΔLogLik), defined as the difference in log likelihood between the model's corresponding GAMM and the baseline GAMM.

In the following subsections, we describe the reading time data used in our study and our procedure for fitting GAMMs.

2.1 Eyetracking Data

The data for our psycholinguistic models come from the English portion of the Dundee Corpus (Kennedy, 2003; Kennedy et al., 2003), a dataset containing naturalistic reading times from an eyetracking study. The data were elicited from ten English-speaking participants reading editorials from British newspaper *The Independent*. The editorials were divided into several *texts*, which were shown to subjects on a screen one at a time. Reading times were obtained for a total of 56,212 tokens, drawn from a vocabulary of 9,776 unique word types, excluding punctuation. Punctuation marks were not treated as separate tokens, but rather as belonging to the words they are attached to.

2.2 GAMMs

Following Goodkind and Bicknell (2018) and Smith and Levy (2013), our GAMMs consist of the following input terms:

- linear terms for the surprisal of the current and previous word;

- tensor product interactions[1] between word length and log (unigram) frequency for the current and previous word;

- a spline[2] term for the current word's position within a text; and

- a binary term representing whether or not the previous word was fixated.

The linear terms for surprisal are excluded from the baseline GAMM. Unigram frequencies were estimated using the One Billion Word Benchmark (LM1B, Chelba et al., 2014). We use the same preprocessing procedure as Goodkind and Bicknell, which removes from the data the first and last words of each text, words preceding punctuation

---

[1]This is a 2-dimensional tensor spline interaction.

[2]Penalized spline regression uses a high-dimensional spline basis to estimate unknown non-linear relations. In order to avoid the over-fitting that otherwise plagues such high-dimensional models, it combines the standard maximum likelihood criterion with a curvature penalty term that biases the regression towards smoother curves.

marks, words containing non-alphabetic characters, words for which no unigram frequency estimate is available, and words following these words. In cases where a word from the Dundee Corpus is tokenized into multiple tokens by a language model, we take the word's surprisal to be the sum of the surprisals for each of the constituent tokens.

Goodkind and Bicknell's GAMM outputs represent predictions for *gaze duration* (GD), defined as the time elapsed between the first fixation on a word token and the first time the subject exits that token. In addition to gaze duration, we train GAMMs to predict two other eyetracking measures: *first fixation duration* (FFD), defined as the time elapsed during the first fixation on a token, and *total duration* (TD), defined as the total amount of time spent looking at a token.

3   Language Modeling

Traditionally, language models form independent components of NLP systems, their outputs serving as inputs to downstream applications. However, following recent advances in transfer learning for NLP, modern neural language models are often designed not to compute word probabilities *per se*, but rather to provide representations of linguistic knowledge that can facilitate training on other tasks (Dai and Le, 2015; Howard and Ruder, 2018). Under this paradigm, a single large neural network is *pre-trained* on a language modeling or other word prediction objective. This pre-trained language model can then be trained, or *fine-tuned*, on another task such as text classification (Yang et al., 2019) or machine translation (Conneau and Lample, 2019). Both kinds of language models are considered in this paper.

3.1   Traditional Language Models

We consider three types of traditional language models: n-gram models, LSTM language models, and Transformer language models. We train four models of each type, with varying numbers of parameters, on the Penn Treebank corpus (Mikolov et al., 2011) and the WikiText-2 corpus (Merity et al., 2016). We additionally train n-gram models on LM1B in order to reproduce and facilitate comparison with Goodkind and Bicknell's (2018) results.

Following Goodkind and Bicknell (2018), our n-gram models were trained using modified Kneser–Ney smoothing with KenLM (Heafield, 2011;

Model	Penn Treebank	WikiText-2
2-Gram	185.7	248.5
3-Gram	148.3	211.1
4-Gram	142.7	206.0
5-Gram	**141.2**	**204.8**
LSTM-200	89.3	106.0
LSTM-425	**85.1**	**98.5**
LSTM-650	89.8	98.8
LSTM-1100	97.9	110.5
Transformer-200	**117.8**	**150.2**
Transformer-424	119.1	151.5
Transformer-650	118.7	154.7
Transformer-1100	119.7	156.6

Table 1: Perplexities attained by our trained models on the Penn Treebank and WikiText-2 testing sets.

Heafield et al., 2013). We trained n-gram models with $n = 2, 3, 4$, and 5 on each dataset. We additionally trained a unigram model in order to populate the word frequency term in the input to the GAMMs.

Our LSTM and Transformer models are based on an implementation publicly available on the official PyTorch website (Paszke et al., 2017).[3] Both models include an embedding layer and a softmax decoding layer. The LSTM model consists of two LSTM layers, while the Transformer model consists of two encoder blocks with masked self-attention, each containing two attention heads. We trained LSTM models with 200, 425, 650, and 1100 hidden units (LSTM-200, -425, -650, and -1100, respectively), as well as Transformer models with 200, 424,[4] 650, and 1100 hidden units (Transformer-200, -424, -650, and -1100, respectively). The embedding size used by each model was equal to its hidden size. For each architecture, training corpus, and hidden size, we trained a model using SGD with the learning rate annealed by .5 when perplexity does not improve on a validation set. Training occurred for a maximum of 50 epochs, stopping early with a patience of 5. The batch size, dropout rate, and initial learning rate were tuned using a Bayesian optimization routine consisting of 7 random trials followed by 13 GPEI trials (Snoek et al., 2012). The LSTM-1100 and Transformer-1100 models were trained using the best hyperparameters for LSTM-650 and Transformer-650, respectively. The testing perplexities attained by our trained models are shown in

---

[3] https://github.com/pytorch/examples/tree/master/word_language_model

[4] Because our Transformer model has two attention heads, it needs to have an even number of hidden units, so we used 424 instead of 425 (like we used in the LSTM).

Table 1.

3.2 Pre-Trained Models

In addition to our traditional language models, we include four pre-trained models in our analysis: GPT-2 (Radford et al., 2019), XLM (Conneau and Lample, 2019), Transformer-XL (Dai et al., 2019), and XLNet (Yang et al., 2019). All four models are variants of Transformer language models but differ from one another in terms of training setup and architectural details. We use the implementations from Hugging Face's *Transformers* library (Wolf et al., 2020) off the shelf, with no fine-tuning. We briefly describe the distinguishing features of each model below.

3.2.1 GPT-2

GPT-2 is a Transformer language model trained on a large corpus called WebText, which was designed to include a diverse array of documents in order to capture domain-general linguistic knowledge. The dataset consists of roughly 8 million webpages obtained from Reddit links. It demonstrates state of the art perplexities on various language modeling testing sets, as well as a notable ability to generate human-like text, especially in the context of summarization. Radford et al. (2019) present GPT-2 models in four sizes; we use the smallest size, which consists of 12 layers, 12 attention heads, and 768 hidden units. GPT-2's vocabulary uses a byte-pair encoding, with 50,257 unique word and sub-word types.

3.2.2 XLM

XLM is similar in approach to GPT-2, but it is specifically designed for cross-lingual language tasks, including multilingual classification and machine translation. The XLM model we use was trained on a combination of English and German Wikipedia entries. It has 6 layers, 1024 hidden units, and 8 attention heads. XLM also uses a byte-pair encoding in its vocabulary, with 64,699 unique word and subword types. Unlike the other models, however, XLM's vocabulary includes German tokens in addition to English tokens.

3.2.3 Transformer-XL

The Transformer-XL model introduces architectural enhancements to the Transformer that facilitate learning of long-distance dependencies. It does this using relative encodings and a segment recurrence mechanism, which augments the Transformer with elements of RNN language models.

Our Transformer-XL model was trained on the WikiText-103 corpus (Merity et al., 2016), and contains 18 layers, 1024 hidden units, and 16 attention heads.

3.2.4 XLNet

Finally, XLNet is a language model that extends Transformer-XL to account for bidirectional context within a language modeling setting. This is achieved using a generalized autoregressive technique, in which words are predicted in a randomized order for each training batch. We use an XLNet model with 12 layers, 768 hidden units, and 12 attention heads, trained on a custom corpus drawn from various sources.

3.3 Language Model Evaluation

We employ two methods for evaluating the outputs of our language models: *perplexity*, the standard evaluation metric for language modeling, and *predictability norm correlation*, our proposed metric for comparing models with different vocabularies.

3.3.1 Perplexity

For a given language model, the perplexity of a text consisting of N tokens is defined by the formula

$$\text{perplexity} = \left(\prod_{i=1}^{N} P(\text{token}_i | \text{tokens}_{j<i}) \right)^{-\frac{1}{N}}$$

where $P(\text{token}_i | \text{tokens}_{j<i})$ is the probability assigned to the ith token after the model has processed the first $i - 1$ tokens. Perplexity can also be defined as the exponential of the average surprisal of the text.

$$\text{perplexity} = e^{-\frac{1}{N} \sum_{i=1}^{N} \ln(P(\text{token}_i | \text{tokens}_{j<i}))}$$

Intuitively, perplexity may be interpreted as the weighted average number of possibilities the language model chooses between when predicting the words in the text. Lower perplexities indicate better language modeling performance, since the model is less uncertain about its predictions. Note that using a larger vocabulary artificially increases perplexity, since the model automatically has more words to choose from, thus decreasing $P(\text{token}_i | \text{tokens}_{j<i})$ on average.

In this study, we calculate the perplexity of each language model on the entire Dundee Corpus, without the preprocessing of Subsection 2.2. All perplexity calculations are based on the tokenization used in Goodkind and Bicknell (2018), which divides the Dundee Corpus into $N = 60{,}916$ tokens. This produces slightly more tokens than the original tokenization used by Kennedy (2003), since punctuation marks are treated as separate tokens, following common practice in language modeling.

3.3.2 Predictability Norm Correlation

As an alternative to perplexity, we evaluate models according to a *predictability norm correlation score* (PNC), defined as the Pearson correlation between surprisal values computed by a language model and surprisal values measured from human subjects using a Cloze task. The data used to calculate PNC come from predictability norms collected by Kennedy et al. (2013) for a 16-sentence subset of the Dundee Corpus. Each subject was shown a random and possibly empty initial segment of each sentence and asked to predict the next word, typing their response into a computer. Predictions were collected from 272 subjects in total, with roughly 25 predictions for each token. The "human" probability values are defined by the proportion of responses for each token that represent correct predictions. Kennedy et al. (2013) report two sets of human probability values: one that counts minor misspellings of the target word as correct predictions, and one that counts them as incorrect. We use the former set of scores.

4   Results

Our results are presented in Table 2 and Figure 1, which show the same data in tabular and graphical form. Overall, GPT-2 outperforms all other models on all metrics, achieving the best perplexity, PNC, and ΔLogLik. Transformer-XL, XL-Net, and the n-gram models trained on LM1B perform significantly better in terms of ΔLogLik than XLM and the models trained on Penn Treebank and WikiText-2. This may be because Penn Treebank and WikiText-2 are significantly smaller than the other training datasets, and because XLM, being a multilingual model, is not as suited to modeling data from native English speakers as the other models.

The models trained on Penn Treebank and WikiText-2 achieve similar levels of ΔLogLik, though the Penn Treebank models generally have a better perplexity while the WikiText-2 models generally have a better PNC. Between LSTMs and Transformers, neither architecture is consistently better than the other in terms of ΔLogLik:

Model	PPL	PNC	ΔLogLik		
			FFD	GD	TD
PRE-TRAINED					
GPT-2	**87.6**	**.633**	**180.9**	**332.7**	**841.2**
XLM	410.3	.155	35.7	95.6	131.3
Trans.-XL	152.6	.566	103.9	183.7	493.7
XLNet	489.2	.580	141.5	259.7	646.0
PENN TREEBANK					
2-Gram	216.9	.300	22.4	27.6	69.0
3-Gram	207.0	.326	24.1	33.2	95.1
4-Gram	206.1	.330	22.5	32.4	95.6
5-Gram	205.7	**.331**	22.4	32.3	96.3
LSTM-200	121.4	.270	49.7	93.9	226.8
LSTM-425	**118.4**	.271	51.3	94.4	238.1
LSTM-650	125.5	.273	**60.8**	**107.7**	**250.3**
LSTM-1100	123.3	.270	47.1	87.9	222.3
Trans.-200	137.5	.277	49.2	88.0	215.6
Trans.-424	144.1	.274	47.8	84.5	209.0
Trans.-650	141.4	.275	51.4	89.0	221.8
Trans.-1100	150.7	.278	44.1	81.8	211.4
WIKITEXT-2					
2-Gram	381.1	.425	19.3	32.6	97.0
3-Gram	364.4	.453	28.2	45.0	125.4
4-Gram	359.8	.455	28.2	45.5	126.6
5-Gram	358.6	.455	28.2	45.9	127.3
LSTM-200	236.5	.443	52.1	93.0	255.7
LSTM-425	**224.4**	.437	49.2	84.8	243.4
LSTM-650	230.5	.436	50.6	84.9	240.6
LSTM-1100	262.3	.450	47.2	84.0	250.9
Trans.-200	319.1	.443	54.4	92.9	251.3
Trans.-424	329.4	**.462**	**61.6**	**104.5**	**279.5**
Trans.-650	340.7	.450	53.6	95.5	271.9
Trans.-1100	337.1	.454	53.9	92.6	261.2
LM1B					
2-Gram	291.1	.506	86.9	149.1	413.6
3-Gram	191.2	.560	122.1	212.2	546.8
4-Gram	172.2	.582	130.5	220.4	552.1
5-Gram	**169.0**	**.583**	131.3	223.4	553.9

Table 2: Perplexity (PPL), PNC, and ΔLogLik.

Penn Treebank LSTMs outperform Penn Treebank Transformers on average, while WikiText-2 Transformers outperform WikiText-2 LSTMs on average. However, controlling for training corpus, our LSTMs are consistently better than our Transformers in terms of perplexity, while our Transformers consistently outperform our LSTMs in terms of PNC.

In the remainder of this section, we describe specific observations about the relationship between language model performance and ΔLogLik.

4.1   Perplexity vs. ΔLogLik

The relationship between perplexity and ΔLogLik is visualized in the top row of Figure 1. Recall that only models trained on the same corpus can be compared with one another in these plots, since the different training corpora have different vocabularies. Indeed, we see a large effect overall of training data on the relationship between perplexity and

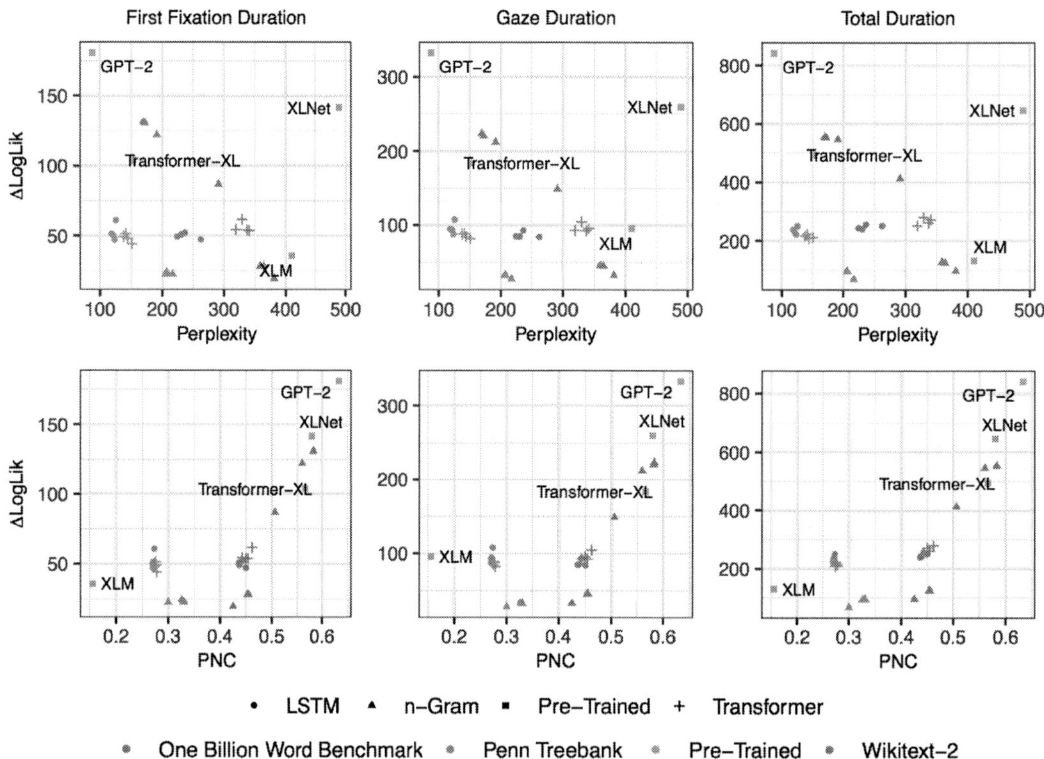

Figure 1: The relationship between language modeling performance and ΔLogLik.

ΔLogLik. Apart from GPT-2 and Transformer-XL, observe that the models trained on the Penn Treebank achieve the lowest perplexities. This likely reflects the fact that the Penn Treebank has the smallest vocabulary among the different models, as well as the fact that the Penn Treebank and the Dundee Corpus are both drawn from newspapers.

For all three eyetracking measures, there appears to be a linear relationship between perplexity and ΔLogLik for different sized n-gram models with the same training corpus, as well as the models trained on the Penn Treebank. However, this relationship does not generalize well to the LSTMs and Transformers trained on WikiText-2. Neither the LSTMs nor the Transformers extrapolate the line that connects the n-gram models. In agreement with Goodkind and Bicknell (2018), we observe that the LSTMs lie below the n-gram line, while the Transformers lie above it. Among models of the same training corpus and architecture, we do not see any relationship between perplexity and ΔLogLik for LSTMs or Transformers trained on WikiText-2.

Because they all use different vocabularies, the pre-trained models cannot be compared with other models in these plots. Nonetheless, XLNet appears to be an outlier among pre-trained models, having the highest perplexity despite achieving the second-highest ΔLogLik for all three eyetracking measures.

Looking across the columns of Figure 1, we observe that the results described in this subsection generalize across all three reading time metrics for the Dundee Corpus.

4.2 PNC vs. ΔLogLik

Next, let us turn to the relationship between PNC and ΔLogLik, visualized on the bottom row of Figure 1. We see a robust relationship in the data, especially among the better models. In particular, the models that achieve a PNC of at least 0.4 show a strong linear relationship between PNC and ΔLogLik. Alternatively, the results may be seen as an exponential or logistic relation that subsumes the models with PNC < 0.4, as ΔLogLik cannot be negative and PNC is capped at 1. Crucially, all of the models with PNC $\geq$ 0.4 are subsumed under the *same trend*, despite the fact that these models collectively use five different vocabularies

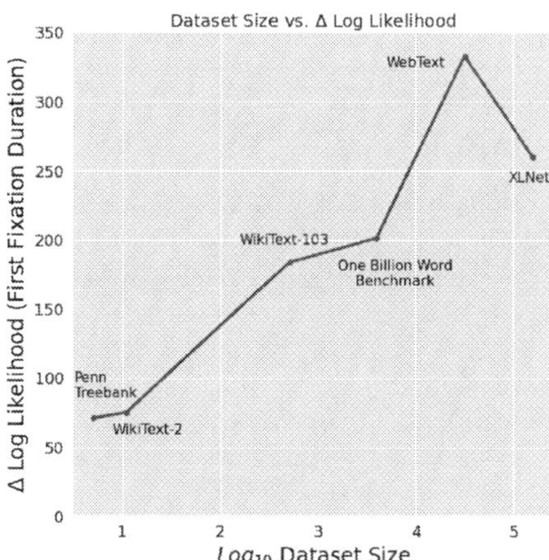

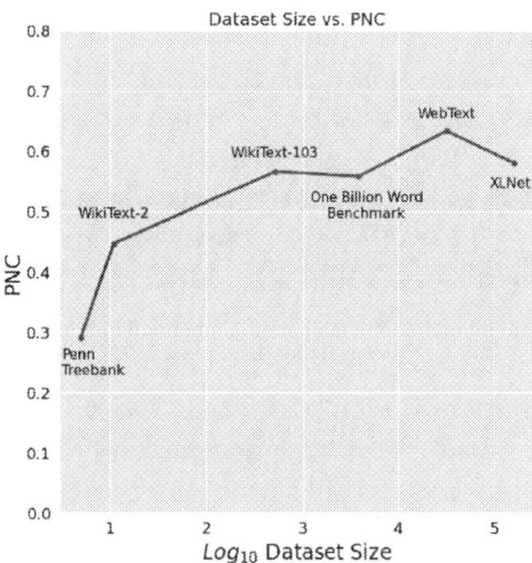

Figure 2: The relationship between training dataset size (MB) and ΔLogLik for monolingual English models. Values are averaged among models trained on the each dataset.

Figure 3: The relationship between training dataset size (MB) and PNC for monolingual English models. Values are averaged among models trained on the each dataset.

of differing sizes. Furthermore, unlike in the case of perplexity, LSTMs do not overperform in terms of PNC relative to their ΔLogLik performance.

Among the pre-trained models, the outlying data point is the XLM model, which achieves the lowest PNC out of all the models. This is unsurprising, considering that XLM is a multilingual model. The other potential outliers are the Penn Treebank data points, which achieve PNCs below 0.4 despite having a similar ΔLogLik to the WikiText-2 models.

As with perplexity, these results generalize across the reading metrics for the Dundee Corpus, though visually speaking, ΔLogLiks based on first fixation duration and total duration appear to provide a bitter fit for an exponential model than gaze duration.

5 Discussion

We focus our discussion on three topics. First, we consider the ways in which each of our experimental variables affects our models' psycholinguistic modeling performance. Next, we briefly identify some properties of PNC as a metric, particularly in terms of its relationship with training corpus size. Finally, we reflect on the implications of our results for language modeling and psycholinguistic modeling evaluation more generally.

5.1 Factors Affecting ΔLogLik

In our experiment, we have analyzed several model architectures, model sizes, and training datasets. Similarly to Merkx and Frank (2020), we determine

that the number of model parameters generally does not significantly impact psycholinguistic modeling performance, whereas model architecture, along with the composition and size of the training corpus, do have a significant impact.

Our findings regarding the effect of model architecture are consistent with the model class effect identified by both Goodkind and Bicknell (2018) and Wilcox et al. (2020), in that LSTMs appear to underperform in terms of ΔLogLik given their perplexities. However, our architecture effect is not as dramatic as the one reported by Wilcox et al.: whereas their n-grams generally show superior psychometric predictive power over their LSTMs, our n-gram models are not on par with that of our LSTMs.

Although our experiment did not control for both training data size and composition separately, we argue that both properties are important factors that affect ΔLogLik. Firstly, notice that the ΔLogLiks for the Penn Treebank LSTMs and Transformers are exceptionally high given that their PNC is less than 0.4, especially the values computed for total duration. Indeed, whereas all other models with PNC < 0.4 achieve ΔLogLiks close to 100 for total duration, the Penn Treebank LSTMs and Transformers exhibit ΔLogLiks in excess of 200. We posit that this phenomenon is due to domain similarity between the newspaper data found in the Penn Treebank and Dundee Corpus datasets, suggesting that the content of the training dataset can improve ΔLogLik even when the amount of data available is small. This is consistent with previous work such as Hale et al. (2019), showing that genre matters when it comes to cognitive modeling. On the other hand, observe that the 3-, 4-, and 5-gram models trained on LM1B outperform Transformer-XL and rival XLNet on ΔLogLik for all three reading time metrics, despite having a much simpler model architecture. Given that LM1B (4 GB) is much bigger than WikiText-103 (515 MB), the training corpus for Transformer-XL, this observation shows that a large dataset can dramatically enhance the psycholinguistic modeling capabilities of an otherwise simple architecture.

It is worth noting that dataset size and quality are both important factors for ΔLogLik. Figure 2 shows the average ΔLogLik for first fixation duration attained by models trained on each dataset, excluding XLM. There, we find that GPT-2 outperforms the other models in terms of psycholinguistic predictive power, including those that are more architecturally sophisticated, namely Transformer-XL and XLNet. Although WebText (40 GB) is not the largest dataset, as it is smaller than XLNet's training corpus (158 GB), it was constructed in a more curated approach than the other datasets. The wide variety of document types included in Web-Text likely makes it a higher-quality training corpus than XLNet's corpus or LM1B, allowing GPT-2 to surpass other models.

5.2 Factors Affecting PNC

Likewise, Figure 3 depicts the relationship between dataset size and PNC. Here, we find that the PNC consistently lies between 0.55 and 0.65 for the larger datasets, but is significantly lower for the smaller datasets. While the lower values for WikiText-2 and Penn Treebank show that smaller datasets generally produce models with lower PNC, the small variance in PNC for the larger datasets is suggestive of diminishing returns in PNC when training corpora are sufficiently large.

Figures 4 and 5 compare PNC to perplexity-based metrics. Figure 4 shows that PNC cannot be predicted from perplexity, highlighting the distinctness of the two metrics. Figure 5 plots the ΔLogLik of gaze duration against *normalized perplexity* (Marti and Bunke, 2001), defined as perplexity divided by vocabulary size. The relationship between normalized perplexity and ΔLogLik appears to be slightly stronger than perplexity alone, but not as strong as the relationship between PNC

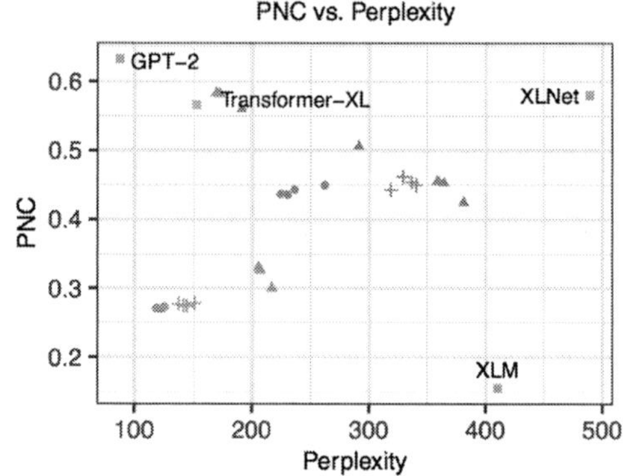

Figure 4: There is no correlation between perplexity and PNC ($\rho = .222$).

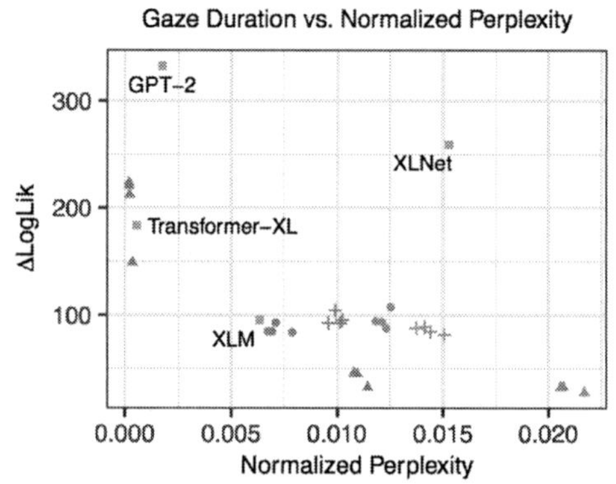

Figure 5: Unlike PNC, normalized perplexity does not exhibit a strong relation with ΔLogLik.

and ΔLogLik. This suggests that the benefits of using PNC over perplexity cannot be replicated simply by adjusting perplexity for differences in vocabulary size.

5.3 Evaluating Surprisal Estimates

While perplexity is the standard metric for evaluating surprisal estimates produced by language models, we have argued throughout this paper that perplexity is not a reliable metric of language modeling performance. In addition to the difficulty presented by perplexity for comparing models with different training conditions, especially pre-trained models, perplexity has been recently shown to be a poor predictor of a language model's ability to capture generalizations about natural language grammar (Ek et al., 2019; Hu et al., 2020). Along those lines, in Figure 4 we have seen that perplexity is a poor predictor of PNC. Taken together, these observations indicate that perplexity does not capture the extent to which language models exhibit human-like behavior. Instead, alternative metrics like PNC or Hu et al.'s (2020) syntactic generalization score explicitly assess the degree to which language models behave like humans, without sensitivity to training conditions or other artifacts of the model.

Our arguments about the reliability of PNC as a measure of language modeling performance raise an interesting question about the role of language models in psycholinguistic modeling. Within the psycholinguistic modeling literature, language models are often viewed as statistical estimators of corpus-based frequencies (e.g., Smith and Levy, 2011). While n-gram models can certainly be understood this way, the complex, increasingly opaque models used in neural NLP do not readily lend themselves to this interpretation. Instead, the literature on pre-training has recast language modeling as a generalization of NLP training objectives (Radford et al., 2019), and pre-trained models have been shown to encode a wide range of linguistic information beyond word and n-gram frequencies (see Rogers et al., 2020 for an overview). Therefore, while Frisson et al. (2005) and Smith and Levy (2011) have argued that corpus-based frequencies are not as suitable for psycholinguistic modeling as Cloze probabilities, our results indicate that pre-trained models with a high PNC such as GPT-2 may capture a notion of predictability that more closely estimates subjective predictability than empirical probabilities, allowing them to serve as better psycholinguistic models.

6 Conclusion

The results reported here suggest that for the purpose of modeling reading times, perplexity does not adequately reveal the relationship between language modeling performance and psycholinguistic modeling performance, especially when vocabulary cannot be controlled for. In contrast, PNC has proven to be a much better predictor of the psychometric capabilities of our language models. This finding is consistent with observations by Frisson et al. (2005) and Smith and Levy (2011) that Cloze probabilities predict self-paced reading times better than corpus probabilities do. In addition to allowing models with different vocabularies to be compared with one another, PNC is much more strongly correlated with psycholinguistic modeling performance than perplexity, as demonstrated by

our results on ΔLogLik. More generally, as there is little to no correlation between perplexity and PNC, PNC can serve as a good supplement to perplexity for language model evaluation, providing information about model behavior that is not captured by the latter.

We have also shown that model architecture, training dataset size, and training dataset composition all contribute substantially to the psycholinguistic modeling capabilities of language models. In particular, the importance of corpus size and composition is reflective of trends in transfer learning, in which advances in downstream NLP tasks are made by using language models to extract general linguistic information from large corpora. Our analysis has shown that large corpora have the potential to provide considerable amounts of linguistic knowledge even through simple model architectures, as in the case of the LM1B n-grams.

As new pre-trained language models are developed, especially with custom vocabularies that make a direct comparison of perplexities impossible, metrics such as PNC can serve as a valuable tool for assessing the quality of language models. In establishing a strong relationship between PNC and ΔLogLik, we have demonstrated that PNC scores convey a psychometrically relevant notion of language model quality that directly measures the degree to which language models exhibit human-like behavior. Reliable metrics like PNC, which are robust to variations in model setup, have the potential to greatly improve our ability to understand the relationship between language models and language.

Acknowledgments

We would like to thank Adam Goodkind, Klinton Bicknell, and Vera Demberg for helping us reproduce Goodkind and Bicknell's (2018) analysis; Alan Kennedy for providing us the Dundee Corpus data; Christopher Geissler for his helpful discussion and assistance in statistical modeling; and the reviewers for their feedback.

References

Christoph Aurnhammer and Stefan Frank. 2019. Comparing Gated and Simple Recurrent Neural Network Architectures as Models of Human Sentence Processing. In *Proceedings of the 41st Annual Conference of the Cognitive Science Society*, pages 112–118, Montreal, Canada. Cognitive Science Society.

Marisa Ferrara Boston, John Hale, Reinhold Kliegl, Umesh Patil, and Shravan Vasishth. 2008. Parsing costs as predictors of reading difficulty: An evaluation using the Potsdam Sentence Corpus. *Journal of Eye Movement Research*, 2(1).

Ciprian Chelba, Tomas Mikolov, Mike Schuster, Qi Ge, Thorsten Brants, Phillipp Koehn, and Tony Robinson. 2014. One Billion Word Benchmark for Measuring Progress in Statistical Language Modeling. *Computing Research Repository*, arXiv:1312.3005.

Alexis Conneau and Guillaume Lample. 2019. Cross-lingual Language Model Pretraining. In *Advances in Neural Information Processing Systems 32*, pages 7059–7069, Vancouver, Canada. Curran Associates, Inc.

Andrew M. Dai and Quoc V. Le. 2015. Semi-supervised Sequence Learning. In *Advances in Neural Information Processing Systems 28*, pages 3079–3087, Montreal, Canada. Curran Associates, Inc.

Zihang Dai, Zhilin Yang, Yiming Yang, Jaime Carbonell, Quoc Le, and Ruslan Salakhutdinov. 2019. Transformer-XL: Attentive Language Models beyond a Fixed-Length Context. In *Proceedings of the 57th Annual Meeting of the Association for Computational Linguistics*, pages 2978–2988, Florence, Italy. Association for Computational Linguistics.

Vera Demberg and Frank Keller. 2008. Data from eye-tracking corpora as evidence for theories of syntactic processing complexity. *Cognition*, 109(2):193–210.

Susan F. Ehrlich and Keith Rayner. 1981. Contextual Effects on Word Perception and Eye Movements during Reading. *Journal of Verbal Learning and Verbal Behavior*, 20(6):641–655.

Adam Ek, Jean-Philippe Bernardy, and Shalom Lappin. 2019. Language Modeling with Syntactic and Semantic Representation for Sentence Acceptability Predictions. In *Proceedings of the 22nd Nordic Conference on Computational Linguistics*, pages 76–85, Turku, Finland. Linköping University Electronic Press.

Stefan Frank. 2009. Surprisal-based comparison between a symbolic and a connectionist model of sentence processing. In *Proceedings of the 31st Annual Conference of the Cognitive Science Society*, pages 1139–1144, Amsterdam, Netherlands. Cognitive Science Society.

Steven Frisson, Keith Rayner, and Martin J. Pickering. 2005. Effects of Contextual Predictability and Transitional Probability on Eye Movements During Reading. *Journal of Experimental Psychology: Learning, Memory, and Cognition*, 31(5):862–877. Place: US Publisher: American Psychological Association.

Adam Goodkind and Klinton Bicknell. 2018. Predictive power of word surprisal for reading times is a linear function of language model quality. In *Proceedings of the 8th Workshop on Cognitive Modeling and Computational Linguistics (CMCL 2018)*, pages 10–18, Salt Lake City, UT. Association for Computational Linguistics.

John Hale. 2001. A Probabilistic Earley Parser as a Psycholinguistic Model. In *Second Meeting of the North American Chapter of the Association for Computational Linguistics*, Pittsburgh, PA. Association for Computational Linguistics.

John Hale, Adhiguna Kuncoro, Keith Hall, Chris Dyer, and Jonathan Brennan. 2019. Text genre and training data size in human-like parsing. In *Proceedings of the 2019 Conference on Empirical Methods in Natural Language Processing and the 9th International Joint Conference on Natural Language Processing (EMNLP-IJCNLP)*, pages 5846–5852, Hong Kong, China. Association for Computational Linguistics.

Kenneth Heafield. 2011. KenLM: Faster and Smaller Language Model Queries. In *Proceedings of the Sixth Workshop on Statistical Machine Translation*, pages 187–197, Edinburgh, United Kingdom. Association for Computational Linguistics.

Kenneth Heafield, Ivan Pouzyrevsky, Jonathan H. Clark, and Philipp Koehn. 2013. Scalable Modified Kneser–Ney Language Model Estimation. In *Proceedings of the 51st Annual Meeting of the Association for Computational Linguistics*, volume 2: Short Papers, pages 690–696, Sofia, Bulgaria. Association for Computational Linguistics.

Sepp Hochreiter and Jürgen Schmidhuber. 1997. Long Short-Term Memory. *Neural Computation*, 9(8):1735–1780.

Jeremy Howard and Sebastian Ruder. 2018. Universal Language Model Fine-tuning for Text Classification. In *Proceedings of the 56th Annual Meeting of the Association for Computational Linguistics*, volume 1: Long Papers, pages 328–339, Melbourne, Australia. Association for Computational Linguistics.

Jennifer Hu, Jon Gauthier, Peng Qian, Ethan Wilcox, and Roger Levy. 2020. A Systematic Assessment of Syntactic Generalization in Neural Language Models. In *Proceedings of the 58th Annual Meeting of the Association for Computational Linguistics*, pages 1725–1744, Seattle, WA. Association for Computational Linguistics.

Dan Jurafsky and James H. Martin. 2008. *Speech and Language Processing: An Introduction to Natural Language Processing, Computational Linguistics, and Speech Recognition*, 2 edition. Prentice Hall Series in Artificial Intelligence. Prentice Hall, Upper Saddle River, NJ.

Alan Kennedy. 2003. The Dundee Corpus. CD-ROM, University of Dundee Department of Psychology, Dundee, United Kingdom.

Alan Kennedy, Robin Hill, and Joël Pynte. 2003. The Dundee Corpus. Poster presented at the 12th European Conference on Eye Movements, Dundee, United Kingdom.

Alan Kennedy, Joël Pynte, Wayne S. Murray, and Shirley-Anne Paul. 2013. Frequency and predictability effects in the Dundee Corpus: An eye movement analysis. *Quarterly Journal of Experimental Psychology*, 66(3):601–618.

Roger Levy. 2008. Expectation-based syntactic comprehension. *Cognition*, 106(3):1126–1177.

U.-V. Marti and H. Bunke. 2001. On the influence of vocabulary size and language models in unconstrained handwritten text recognition. In *Proceedings of Sixth International Conference on Document Analysis and Recognition*, pages 260–265, Seattle, WA. IEEE.

Stephen Merity, Caiming Xiong, James Bradbury, and Richard Socher. 2016. Pointer Sentinel Mixture Models. In *ICLR 2017 Conference Track*, Toulon, France. OpenReview.

Danny Merkx and Stefan L. Frank. 2020. Comparing Transformers and RNNs on predicting human sentence processing data. *Computing Research Repository*, arXiv:2005.09471.

Tomáš Mikolov, Anoop Deoras, Stefan Kombrink, Lukáš Burget, and Jan Černocký. 2011. Empirical Evaluation and Combination of Advanced Language Modeling Techniques. In *INTERSPEECH-2011*, pages 605–608, Florence, Italy. International Speech Communication Association.

Jeff Mitchell, Mirella Lapata, Vera Demberg, and Frank Keller. 2010. Syntactic and Semantic Factors in Processing Difficulty: An Integrated Measure. In *Proceedings of the 48th Annual Meeting of the Association for Computational Linguistics*, pages 196–206, Uppsala, Sweden. Association for Computational Linguistics.

Irene Fernandez Monsalve, Stefan L. Frank, and Gabriella Vigliocco. 2012. Lexical surprisal as a general predictor of reading time. In *Proceedings of the 13th Conference of the European Chapter of the Association for Computational Linguistics*, pages 398–408, Avignon, France. Association for Computational Linguistics.

Adam Paszke, Sam Gross, Soumith Chintala, Gregory Chanan, Edward Yang, Zachary DeVito, Zeming Lin, Alban Desmaison, Luca Antiga, and Adam Lerer. 2017. Automatic differentiation in PyTorch. In *NIPS 2017 Autodiff Workshop*, Long Beach, CA. OpenReview.

Alec Radford, Jeffrey Wu, Rewon Child, David Luan, Dario Amodei, and Ilya Sutskever. 2019. Language Models are Unsupervised Multitask Learners. Technical Report, OpenAI, San Francisco, CA.

Brian Roark, Asaf Bachrach, Carlos Cardenas, and Christophe Pallier. 2009. Deriving lexical and syntactic expectation-based measures for psycholinguistic modeling via incremental top-down parsing. In *Proceedings of the 2009 Conference on Empirical Methods in Natural Language Processing*, pages 324–333, Singapore. Association for Computational Linguistics.

Anna Rogers, Olga Kovaleva, and Anna Rumshisky. 2020. A Primer in BERTology: What we know about how BERT works. *Computing Research Repository*, arXiv:2002.12327.

Nathaniel Smith and Roger Levy. 2011. Cloze but no cigar: The complex relationship between cloze, corpus, and subjective probabilities in language processing. In *Expanding the Space of Cognitive Science: Proceedings of the 33rd Annual Meeting of the Cognitive Science Society*, pages 1637–1642, Boston, MA. Cognitive Science Society.

Nathaniel J. Smith and Roger Levy. 2013. The effect of word predictability on reading time is logarithmic. *Cognition*, 128(3):302–319.

Jasper Snoek, Hugo Larochelle, and Ryan P Adams. 2012. Practical Bayesian Optimization of Machine Learning Algorithms. In *Advances in Neural Information Processing Systems 25*, pages 2951–2959, Lake Tahoe, NV. Curran Associates, Inc.

Wilson L. Taylor. 1953. "Cloze Procedure": A New Tool for Measuring Readability. *Journalism Quarterly*, 30(4):415–433.

Ashish Vaswani, Noam Shazeer, Niki Parmar, Jakob Uszkoreit, Llion Jones, Aidan N. Gomez, Łukasz Kaiser, and Illia Polosukhin. 2017. Attention is All you Need. In *Advances in Neural Information Processing Systems 30*, pages 5998–6008, Long Beach, CA. Curran Associates, Inc.

Ethan Gotlieb Wilcox, Jon Gauthier, Jennifer Hu, Peng Qian, and Roger Levy. 2020. On the Predictive Power of Neural Language Models for Human Real-Time Comprehension Behavior. *Computing Research Repository*, arXiv:2006.01912.

Thomas Wolf, Lysandre Debut, Victor Sanh, Julien Chaumond, Clement Delangue, Anthony Moi, Pierric Cistac, Tim Rault, Rémi Louf, Morgan Funtowicz, Joe Davison, Sam Shleifer, Patrick von Platen, Clara Ma, Yacine Jernite, Julien Plu, Canwen Xu, Teven Le Scao, Sylvain Gugger, Mariama Drame, Quentin Lhoest, and Alexander M. Rush. 2020. HuggingFace's Transformers: State-of-the-art Natural Language Processing. *Computing Research Repository*, arXiv:1910.03771.

Simon N. Wood. 2004. Stable and Efficient Multiple Smoothing Parameter Estimation for Generalized Additive Models. *Journal of the American Statistical Association*, 99(467):673–686.

Zhilin Yang, Zihang Dai, Yiming Yang, Jaime Carbonell, Russ R. Salakhutdinov, and Quoc V. Le. 2019. XLNet: Generalized Autoregressive Pretraining for Language Understanding. In *Advances in Neural Information Processing Systems 32*, pages 5753–5763, Vancouver, Canada. Curran Associates, Inc.

David Zola. 1981. The Effect of Redundancy on the Perception of Words in Reading. Technical Report 216, University of Illinois at Urbana-Champaign Center for the Study of Reading, Champaign, IL.

David Zola. 1984. Redundancy and word perception during reading. *Perception & Psychophysics*, 36(3):277–284.

Association for Computational Linguistics
209 N. Eighth Street
Stroudsburg, Pennsylvania 18360

ISBN 978-1-7138-1991-2